BURPEE

TOMATOES

Robert Hendrickson

Macmillan•USA

For Marilyn

When you walk into the garden,

the roses (and tomatoes) jealously

whisper your name.

MACMILLAN
A Simon & Schuster Macmillan Company
1633 Broadway
New York, NY 10019

MACMILLAN is a registered trademark of Macmillan, Inc.
BURPEE is a registered trademark of W. Atlee Burpee & Company.
Library of Congress Cataloging-in-Publication Data is available on request.

ISBN: 0-02-861607-3

Manufactured in the United States of America.

10 9 8 7 6 5 4 3 2 1

Interior Design by Nick Anderson

Photography courtesy of W. Atlee Burpee & Company.

Contents

The Bite Heard 'Round the World

Today the tomato is America's favorite home-grown food—four out of five vegetable gardeners grow tomatoes in their gardens—but it has not always enjoyed such widespread popularity. Although tomatoes had been growing in the Americas for thousands of years, the tomato had come to be known alternately as a powerful aphrodisiac and as a deadly poisonous fruit. Native to South America and grown in the Andes, tomatoes were first cultivated by the Mayans throughout Central America. The tomato plants bore clusters of tiny fruit no bigger than marbles on a small, sparse vine and were called *xtomati* by the Mayans who brought them to the great market of Chichén Itzá in Mexico. Cortez and his band of conquistadors, seeing a good thing, carried the *xtomatl* seeds back with them to Spain—along with the rest of their New World plunder—where the tomato found wide acceptance among the Spanish and later, with other Mediterranean peoples.

But soon the tomato began to run into trouble. Perhaps because the plant hailed from exotic climes and bore a luscious, shapely, scarlet fruit, tomatoes became known as potent aphrodisiacs and acquired the name of "love apples." The tomato is still called *Liebesapfel* (love apple)

Fruit or Vegetable?

Botanically, the tomato is a fruit or berry (it contains seeds) belonging to the nightshade family. Legally, the tomato is generally considered a vegetable. This determination was made in 1893 when an importer contended that the tomato was a fruit and, therefore, not subject to vegetable import duties. The U.S. Supreme Court held that the tomato had to be considered a vegetable when it was served in a soup or with the main course of a meal. The Court allowed it to be considered a fruit when eaten out of hand or as dessert. Scientists, of course, did not consider this legal reasoning and so we are stuck with the inconsistency today.

today in Germany. That they were known as "love apples" at all may have its origin in the story of the Frenchman who misheard the Italian pronounce *Pomi dei Mors* or Moor's apples, as they were commonly called in Spain. The Frenchman thought he said *pommes d'amour* (apples of love). Or so the story goes. Then again, the tomato's reputation as an aphrodisiac may have come from its resemblance to the human heart, the "seat of love" for the ancients.

But just as quickly as the love-apple reputation arose, another arose, too: That tomatoes were deadly poisonous. Both labels, we now know, were wrong—tomatoes are neither poisonous nor, unfortunately, imbued with wondrous aphrodisiac qualities. Though the tomato itself was a perfectly healthful fruit, the stigma had been placed and it would be another century before tomatoes would be grown for their luscious fruits in England and northern parts of Europe. Tomatoes are, botanically speaking, members of the nightshade or Solanaceae family, which includes many poisonous plant species. While the tomato fruits are quite safe to eat, other parts of the tomato plant do contain poisonous alkaloids.

The tomato continued to fascinate and repel. Noted English traveler John Gerard wrote in his sixteenth-century Herbal that "these Apples of Love yield very little nourishment to the body and the same naught and corrupt."

The horticulturist Philip Miller, a colleague of the great Linnaeus (Carolus Linnaeus, a Sweedish botanist, founded the binomial nomenclature that is the basis of modern taxonomy), observed there were those who thought that "the nourishment [tomatoes] afford must be bad."

For years, love apples were cultivated solely as ornamentals in greenhouses in northern Europe and England, and their negative reputation spread back to the United States, where the tomato plant was only grown as a curiosity until well into the nineteenth century. They were considered by all accounts to be poisonous, and perhaps were too scarlet and shapely for the Puritan palate: Virtuous maidens did not eat of this fruit. It continued to find its place, though, and was used as a folk remedy, "applied externally to remove eruptions upon the skin."

It is recorded that the tomato was grown in Thomas Jefferson's garden at Monticello in 1781, and tomatoes were featured in George Washington's gardens at Mount Vernon, but were strictly ornamental. The New Orleans market offered them to more knowing housewives of French descent as early as 1812. Yankee sea captains introduced tomatoes to New England and Philadelphia, where housewives used them to make "ketch" or "ketchup." But beyond this, the tomato was little known.

I Say...

"You say toe-may-toe and I say toe-mah-toe," Cole Porter wrote, and he might have added that Americans also pronounce the fruit "tamater," "termater," "mater," "tomarters," and "tomaties," among other variations. Regional pronunciations of the plural tomatoes are even stranger, including, "tomatussis" and "martisses." Those who, like the English, pronounce the fruit "toe-mah-toe" are probably more historically correct. The fruit was first called "tomate" in Spain and pronounced in three syllables. The final "o," incidentally, has no place at all in "tomato," appearing there only because nineteenth-century Englishmen erroneously believed that it should have this common Spanish ending.

The tomato finally began to find acceptance around 1835, when it began appearing in markets across the land. The editor of the *Maine Farmer* wrote that tomatoes were "a useful article of diet and should be found on everyone's table." Recipes for tomatoes appeared in homemaking magazines, home gardeners began growing them, and nurseries began offering different varieties. "Tomatoes can be prepared in so many delicious ways that one can eat them every day and not get tired of them," wrote the eminently respectable botanist George Washington Carver.

You Put WHAT in My Clam Chowder??

Tomatoes are commonly used in clam chowder, everywhere but in New England, that is. There the prejudice is so strong for a milk-based clam chowder that in 1939 Maine lawmaker John Seeder introduced a bill into the state legislature making it illegal to add tomatoes to chowder within the State of Maine. Violators of the proposed law would have been sentenced to digging a barrel of clams at high tide (i.e., underwater, for you non-bluenoses).

That was, of course, many years ago, and today we find tomatoes everywhere. Unfortunately, the supermarket version shares only the name with homegrown tomatoes. Those rocklike, flannel-textured, commercially grown specimens in supermarkets are bred and grown for uniformity of size, for easier machine harvesting, and for skin toughness, so that they will ship and keep well. But commercial tomatoes are not grown for flavor. Even commercial varieties of tomatoes are too soft to travel well, so the tomatoes are picked as soon as they are full-grown, but still as green as grass. These green tomatoes are ripened with ethylene gas, an artificial process that not only detracts from their flavor, but also deprives them of their vitamin C content. The end result is a pale shadow of a vine-ripened tomato.

Fortunately, growing tomatoes is one of life's great pleasures. To the great good luck of all, tomatoes can be grown abundantly almost anywhere—in vegetable gardens, on front lawns and patios, even high up in skyscraper window boxes. This book is dedicated to tomato-lovers everywhere, and everything you need to know to grow them is in this book. Happy growing!

Chapter 1

Planning for Tomatoes

Tomato plants can be grown just about anywhere: In the traditional vegetable garden, tomato patch, and flower bed; in containers on the porch, patio, terrace, or deck; or even in windowboxes. Suburban gardeners may find a place for the garden bed in a strip along the driveway, and those gardeners with limited sun for their garden may want to try to grow tomatoes even in partial shade. Although tomatoes are sunlovers, you'll get some tomatoes anyway, even if not a bountiful harvest. Tomato plants also grow well in the vertical garden, great for gardeners with limited space because tomatoes can grow on fences, trellises, or a lattice on the house or garage wall. Of course, you can also convert your front lawn into a tomato patch. With a little imagination, your tomatoes can fit in anywhere and add beauty to just about any landscape.

An existing lattice-work fence can be a great place to grow a bumper crop of tomatoes, such as the 'Big Boy Hybrid' shown here.

TOMATOES
IN THE GARDEN

The vegetable garden is the obvious place to grow your tomatoes. Plant them in rows along with lettuce, radishes, beans, onions, beets, carrots, cabbages, peppers, and almost any vegetable that doesn't take up a great deal of space.

Vertical Gardening

Not long ago, a gardener in Athens, Georgia, grew 230 tomato plants in exactly one square yard of garden space. He built a 27-foot-high tower spiked with planting holes, filled the holes with rich compost, and fashioned a long, perforated pipe down the center of the tower through which to water the plants. He had to cultivate the plants—that is, to water and to pick the tomatoes—from atop a ladder, but the Georgia gardener's vertical tomato patch equaled about 800 feet of conventional garden space and yielded hundreds of tomatoes. If space is your concern, you might consider a vertical garden, too. You can easily make your tower smaller than his by using the strawberry pyramids available at most nurseries.

In the Herb Garden

Many herbs, such as chives and parsley, grow well next to tomato plants. You might also want to set basil near them, for there is hardly a tomato dish that isn't improved by a bit of basil, "the tomato herb." Chervil, dill, marjoram, oregano, sage, and tarragon are other herbs called for in many tomato recipes. Rocket, also known as arugula, is especially delicious with tomatoes.

In the Kitchen Garden

You can also create a kitchen garden, planting many wonderful herbs and vegetables and some fast-growing annuals such as cosmos, marigolds, sunflowers, and petunias. Don't forget to plant edible flowers, such as peppery nasturtiums, violets, pansies, roses, and scented geraniums.

'Big Girl Hybrid'

Tomatoes and Sunflowers

You'll learn in Chapter 2 about staking tomato plants and, as luck would have it, the sunflower plant makes a natural, sturdy stake for tomatoes. Besides that, sunflowers look great next to tomatoes and also provide shade, helping to prevent sun-scalded fruit. Plant sunflowers close to your tomatoes about the same time you set out your tomato plants.

Tomatoes as Ornamentals

Instead of adding ornamentals to your tomato patch, try adding tomatoes to your ornamental garden. Many tomato plants can do double duty in the flower border and look quite attractive with annuals and perennials. Some particularly eye-catching tomato plants to grow for their beauty alone are the green-and-white striped tomatoes and the bronze-leaved Abraham Lincoln varieties.

When combining tomatoes with ornamentals, keep in mind that plants of the same height are often planted together for the best visual effect. Taller plants, in general, belong in the rear of the garden. Pairing tall sunflowers with certain tall varieties of tomatoes makes a handsome display. Smaller, indeterminate tomato types are best for the middle of the border, and the smallest cocktail tomatoes can be used as edging plants.

SOME PLACES TO AVOID

Below are some places you should not plant your tomatoes, either because the locations may be inconvenient for you or unsuitable for the tomato plants.

Secluded Areas

Avoid secluded or distant areas where you may neglect them. Choose a site that is easily accessible from the house and near a water source so that you can easily use a hose or carry buckets of water to the garden. Garden tools and supplies should be stored nearby.

Busy Roads

Locate the tomato patch away from any heavily trafficked roads bordering your property. Exhaust fumes stunt plant growth and sometimes kill tomato plants. A fence will help, but it won't be totally effective. A dense hedge would be more effective.

Certain Trees

Keep tomato plants 40 to 50 feet away from shallow-rooted trees, such as maples, elms, willows, and poplars, although deep-rooted trees such as oaks present less of a problem. The feeder roots of trees grow out as far sideways as the branches grow out, and the roots can rob garden soil of moisture and nutrients. If tomato plants can't be kept far enough away because of space limitations, dig a narrow trench about three feet deep between the garden and the trees bordering it. Line one side of the trench with galvanized sheet metal or heavy plastic, and refill the trench with soil. The roots will take years to work their way through this barrier and root pruning won't hurt the trees. It is especially important not to plant tomatoes near black walnut trees or English walnuts grafted onto the roots of black walnut trees because the roots of this species produce a substance called "juglone," which stunts tomato growth. The black walnut roots exude juglone as far out as the roots extend.

Bad Companions

Some vegetables and herbs aren't good compan-

ions for tomatoes. For example, potatoes, eggplants, and peppers share many of the same diseases, and tomatoes don't seem to grow well alongside fennel and kohlrabi.

This landscape-tie raised bed will produce lots of juicy tomatoes, while requiring very little maintenance. The black plastic will warm the soil quickly in the spring, speeding up harvest, and making weeding chores almost nonexistent. The soil in the raised bed drains well and stays loose for the plants' roots. Finally, the mulched paths make for easy, mud-free harvesting in any weather, and don't need any weeding or mowing.

MAKING A RAISED BED

Raised beds can be ideal for tomatoes because these beds ensure good soil drainage and keep the soil from compacting. Construct the raised beds no wider than 4 feet across so that you can reach easily into the middle of the bed from all sides without actually stepping into it. To hold the bed neatly together, the walls of the raised bed can be built of wood, stone, or even concrete, or you can have no walls at all—just let the sides of the bed slope down naturally. Organic gardeners avoid pressure-treated wood because it has been treated with poisonous chemicals that leach in the soil, contaminating the soil and the plants. In the end, a wise choice for material in a raised bed might be "plastic lumber," made from recycled plastic. Plastic lumber tends to stay good-looking for a long time.

SELECTING PLANTS

You'll want to choose healthy-looking, dark green, stocky plants of a named variety. You'll find the greatest selection at a good garden center or greenhouse. Avoid plants that already have flowers or fruit, unless they are planted in pots six inches or larger. Plants with flowers or fruit rarely yield as much in the long run as plants that are set out before they start flowering. You should also avoid plants with spotted or yellowed leaves because there is no sense in bringing home potential disease and pest problems.

DIRECT-SEEDING TOMATOES

Most tomatoes take a long time to fruit from seed so they must be started indoors and planted

Instant Tomato Patch

To convert an area of lawn into an almost-instant tomato patch, follow these simple steps: In early spring, mow the grass as short as possible. Spread about three inches of decayed leaves, clippings, or compost over the patch. Cover the area with black plastic, then a layer of attractive mulch, such as shredded bark. After the compost has settled down (about one week), make planting holes about two feet apart, and set the plants in the holes. The turf grass, leaves, and clippings quickly decompose under the plastic, creating rich soil for your plants. You may also want to companion-plant your tomato patch with marigolds—these will help combat the meadow nematode.

out once the weather warms up in the spring. But several tomatoes are recommended for seeding directly into the ground. Among these are the 'Fireball,' 'New Yorker,' 'Coldset,' and 'Subartic' varieties. 'Johnny Jump-up' is said to produce all its crop in 100 days from planting the seed in the garden. Plant them right where they will grow at the same time you transplant out seedlings.

CONTAINER GARDENING

Containers are a great choice for gardeners with limited space and gardening time. Potting up containers may be less time-consuming than preparing a new garden bed, but plants in containers still require attention. Start a container garden by picking the right containers and the sunniest spot for your pots and planters. Tomatoes ideally need at least six hours of sun a day. Container plants require more water than plants in the ground. You must also use the correct hand tools for your container garden—these include a trowel for planting and a small cultivator to use on top of the soil to prevent a crust from forming.

Apartment or condo dwellers and others without planting space can also harvest fresh, garden-ripe tomatoes by growing tomatoes in containers. Anyone with a sunny windowsill, balcony, patio, fire escape, roof, porch, or doorstep has space for a tomato minigarden. In fact, of all vegetables, tomatoes probably offer the largest edible reward for the time and effort spent in container gardening.

THE RIGHT CONTAINER FOR YOUR TOMATOES

Just about any large container is suitable for tomatoes. Imaginative gardeners have used decorative urns, bushel baskets, vegetable crates, wooden barrels, large earthenware urns, butter tubs, wastepaper baskets, wine casks, wheelbarrows, and strawberry barrels. Of course, you can always use clay pots, cement planters, hanging baskets,

and the ever-popular and economical plastic pots. Depending on your aesthetic taste, your containers may be very attractive or very plain, the latter including plastic milk containers, trash bins, and laundry baskets. The plainest container of all would be a large plastic bag of potting soil. Just lay it down, cut an "x" in the top, and plant. Nothing could be easier. Many gardeners also construct their own containers from woods such as redwood, cedar, or cypress, which won't rot easily, or even from thin plywood.

Growing 'Tumbler' in a decorative urn

Remember that all container materials are not created equal. Clay, wood, and cement are more porous than plastic and fiberglass, and plants in these nonporous containers will need more watering.

Container Requirements

When growing the smaller tomato varieties, look for containers that can hold at least one gallon of soil, or the equivalent capacity of an 8-inch clay pot. For larger tomatoes, use containers that hold at least two gallons of soil, or the equivalent capacity of a 10-inch clay pot. For the large, spreading varieties, the larger the container, the better. Use at least a 2 foot × 2 foot × 2 foot container.

All tomato containers must have large drainage holes in the bottom. To prevent the soil from leaking out through the drainage holes, line the bottom with a scrap of screen or burlap. Let air circulate beneath the drainage hole by elevating the container slightly on bricks or boards. Hanging baskets and windowboxes must be securely fastened—planters get very heavy when full of moist soil.

The Right Growing Mix for Your Plants

Garden soil alone is not a good growing medium for plants in containers because it can compact easily, preventing water and air from moving freely, and because it also can contain pests and diseases. Good potting soils are very light so that they drain freely and hold moisture. "Soilless" mixes of vermiculite, perlite, and peat most, as well as potting soils with bark and sand are good choices. Because these soil mixes do not include nutrients, you must add nutrients yourself. Potting soils are readily available in nurseries and garden centers, or you can make your potting soil by combining the ingredients above for a soilless mix. Alternatively, try one of the mixes listed below.

Compost Mix

Mix together equal parts of compost, builder's sand, and good garden soil. Add a handful of cottonseed meal.

USDA Soilless Fertilizer Mix

Add one bushel each of horticultural-grade vermiculite and peat moss to 14 ounces of ground dolomitic limestone, 4 ounces of 20 percent superphosphate, and 8 ounces of 5-10-5 fertilizer. Mix thoroughly, adding water while combining ingredients to keep down the dust. This mix is highly recommended and easy to work with. Its lightness makes it by far the best soil for hanging baskets or window boxes.

Always moisten the potting soil with water before adding it to the container to remove air bubbles and pockets. Fill the container with the moistened mixture up to one inch from the top. You probably want to fill all the containers except the smallest ones where you want them to stand—filled containers are very heavy.

Choosing Your Container Tomatoes

Any of the larger tomato varieties grow well in containers. You will also find a number of midget varieties suitable for container planting. These include 'Small Fry,' excellent staked in a small container because it grows about 3 feet tall. 'Tiny Tim,' which grows only 8 inches to 15 inches tall, and 'Toy Boy' do well falling naturally from a hanging basket.

Many tomato plants are ideal for growing in containers, such as the 'Sweet 100' plant.

Planting and Staking

For containers, you may plant tomatoes, either raised from seed or bought from a nursery, in the same manner as you would set transplants into the garden. Stake all plants except the shorter varieties or those in hanging baskets. Almost all the staking methods given in Chapter 4 can be adapted to container planting. You can make a "tomato tree" in a basket by shaping a cylinder of concrete

Patio and Window Box Varieties

Miniature tomatoes are valuable for the window box and hanging basket, and all small-space gardens because they grow on plants only one foot tall. These midget tomatoes range in shape from cherry and plum types to the egg-shaped tomatoes. The size of both plant and fruit were considered in selecting the varieties recommended here. Often these midgets will bear up to 200 little fruits on a single plant:

'Basket Pak'	'Red Cherry'
'Burgess Early Salad'	'Red Peach'
'Burpee Tumbler Hybrid'	'Red Pear'
'Droplet'	'Red Plum'
'Dwarf Champion'	'Saladette'
'Early Red Cherry'	'Small Fry'
'Early Salad'	'Stokes Alaska'
'Epoch Dwarf Bush'	'Subarctic'
'Gardener's Delight'	'Sugar Lump'
'German Dwarf Bush Imp'	'Sugar Red'
'Grape Tomato'	'Sugar Yellow'
'Hybrid Pickle'	'Super Sweet
'Johnny Jump-up'	100 Hybrid'
'Merit'	'Tiny Tim'
'Patio'	'Tom Tom'
'Pixie Hybrid'	'Toy Boy'
'Porter'	'Tumbling Tom'
'Presto'	'Window Box'
'Pretty Patio'	'Yellow Pear'
'Red Currant'	'Yellow Tiny Tim'

reinforcing wire into a large "basket." Or you can train plants up an adjoining fence or wall. Staking will provide more room for plants to grow and they'll be easier to care for and far more attractive. It's a good idea to place your stakes in the container when you're potting up. This minimizes the chance of damaging plant roots at a later stage.

Watering

Tomato plants in containers need more water than plants grown in the garden and must be watered whenever you find the soil dry down to $1/8$-inch deep. This means you may have to water three or four times a week during hot, dry weather. But don't overwater or let your plants stand in water overnight. The best time to water is early in the morning. But there are several times you should avoid watering: Late in the evening because you don't want the leaves to stay wet all night—that encourages plant disease—and in the middle of the day when plants are transpiring. You should also make certain that the water is reaching the bottom of the pot. You can do this by inserting a drainpipe from the soil line to the bottom of the container. Fill the pipe with builder's sand and pour water into it so that water will always reach the roots.

Fertilizing

The fertilizer in the soil mix will support plant growth for about six weeks. After that time, use half-strength, diluted liquid or feed plants once a week with a solution of one tablespoon of water-soluble fertilizer per gallon of water. Be careful not to use too much nitrogenous fertilizer. If you want to use dry fertilizer, sprinkle one level teaspoon of 5-10-5 fertilizer per square foot over the surface of soil every three weeks.

Pollination

If your plant flowers but doesn't set fruit, there may not be enough wind to effect pollination. Gently shake the plant once a day to help it along.

General Care

Container-grown tomato plants are subject to the same diseases, insects, and disorders as plants grown in the garden and should be cared for in the same way. To limit potential problems, avoid overcrowding tomato plants in containers. They need the same amount of space as garden-grown tomatoes.

Look Beyond Your Borders

Consider renting land for a tomato patch if you haven't got enough for the garden you want. Some cities offer gardeners this opportunity at a minimal cost. There are also community gardens in many cities that offer plots to resident gardeners. Another possibility is renting a vacant lot from a private owner whose land lies idle. They'll probably be glad for the care and attention you'll give their land, not to mention the beauty your tomato patch will add.

Chapter 2

Planting and Growing Guide

Tomatoes will grow just about anywhere if the right varieties are planted at the right time and receive proper care and attention. For a bountiful harvest of healthy tomatoes, take steps to provide your plants with

their light, water, and nutritional needs. Tomatoes will actually bear crops in many types of soil and in many locations, but you'll get the best results if you can provide the ideal conditions for the plants.

LOCATION

Sun

Tomatoes should ideally occupy the sunniest spot in the garden, where they receive at least 6 to 8 hours of direct sunlight daily, preferably in the middle of the day. When grown in full sun, tomatoes will grow, taste, and look better, be subject to fewer diseases and insect problems, and yield far more fruit than if planted in the shade. Tomatoes raised in full sun will even have a higher vitamin C content.

The tomato is definitely a sun-loving plant, one that is commonly called a "long-day" plant, but this is not to say that tomatoes can't be grown well in much less direct sunlight. Tomatoes grown in partial shade will yield fruit but will yield less fruit over a longer period of time. Many gardeners forced to plant in half-sun have raised tomato plants yielding 10 to 20 fruits on a bush. That yield is, of course, small compared with plants set in the sun, which routinely bear 12 to 20 fruits and can yield up to 200 tomatoes. A bit of shade may actually be good for tomato plants grown in extremely hot, southern climates. Commercial growers often plant their tomatoes only 14 inches apart so the blossoms get a bit of shade and fewer flowers drop off during hot spells. Blossoms drop off when day temperatures rise above 90°F and night temperatures exceed 85°F. Shade also keeps tomato roots cool and helps protect developing fruits from sunscald. Contrary to popular belief, intense direct sunlight doesn't redden tomatoes but burns them yellow. Shade in very hot areas can even help prevent uneven coloring of tomato fruits, as the red pigment in tomatoes often won't form when temperatures exceed 85°F.

Certainly don't give up if your property is very shady. Experiment. Try different varieties, especially early-bearing types that will get plenty of sun before the trees leaf out. But as a general rule, plant your tomatoes in as much sunlight as you have.

Where to Plant Your Plants

Tomatoes planted in a warm microclimate such as on a southerly or southeasterly slope—where the springtime sun falls a little more directly than on a level surface—is the ideal place for your plants. The soil temperature rises here faster than elsewhere, helping the tomatoes get off to a good start.

A sloping site will also provide the air circulation so important to tomatoes because as air cools, it flows downhill, creating a current. If you can find a sloping southerly spot for your plants that is also against a garden wall, house, or garage, so much the better. One way to create a microclimate and simulate the effect of a garden wall is to plant a dense row of pole beans northwest of the tomato rows. Protected from wind and warmed by a wall, the tomatoes will bear earlier and as much as eight weeks longer than other tomato plants.

SOIL

Most "tomatologists" claim that the ideal soil for early tomato varieties is a sandy loam—that is, a soil which contains a large proportion of sand, but which has enough silt and clay to make it hold together. Squeezed when moist, sandy loam will form a ball that holds together without breaking. Sandy loam is doubtless the best soil for all-around garden purposes and is ideal where early planting is the prime consideration. It can be worked almost as early in the season as sandy soil, and it retains much more moisture and nutrients than do sands.

For main-season and late tomatoes, a loamy soil is usually preferred. Loamy soil retains even more moisture and nutrients than sandy loam does, and if you squeeze it in your hand when it is dry, it will form a ball. Because loamy soils hold moisture better, blossom end rot is less likely to occur on fruits grown in these soils. This disease is caused, in part, by a fluctuation in water supply—that is, dry weather one week, wet the next.

Of course even if your soil isn't one of these types, you can still grow tomatoes. Add generous amounts of compost to help improve sandy or clay-rich soil.

Fertility

If your garden soil is healthy—other plants in your yard are doing fine—you can set the plants out and see how well they do the first year. Unless the soil is very poor on your property, you'll get a yield ranging anywhere from fair to excellent. Otherwise you can take soil samples before planting time and have them tested by your state agricultural extension service or a commercial laboratory. You can also find inexpensive, do-it-yourself soil-test kits at many garden centers.

Soil Testing

One of the most important results this test will give you is the pH of your soil. The pH factor expresses the acidity or alkalinity (so-called "sourness" or "sweetness") of soil. The pH scale runs from 0 (very acidic) to 14 (very alkaline), with pH 7 representing a neutral number—the lower numbers are acid, the larger numbers are alkaline. Most plants grow best in the neutral range, somewhere between 6.5 and 7.5 pH. However, the tomato is a moderately acid-sensitive vegetable that can be grown successfully in a pH range of pH 5.5 to pH 6.8, with a value near pH 6.8 considered best. Your pH test kit or lab results will include instructions on how to correct your soil if it is too acid or alkaline. Agricultural-grade, ground limestone sold as lime is usually added if a soil is too acid. Aluminum sulfate, or organic materials such as sulfur, sawdust, oak leaves, and cottonseed meal are added if the soil is too alkaline. Specific application rates will be recommended by the testing service.

Drainage

Good drainage is imperative for tomatoes because they do not thrive with "wet feet"—that is, when their roots soak in water. Good drainage means that water passes through the soil, not over it, and that it does not collect or bead up on the surface. Water should move through the soil quickly, never completely blocking the movement of air through the soil. If you're not sure whether your soil drains properly, select a section and dig a hole 1 foot deep. Fill the hole to the top with water. If the water is gone in fewer than 2 hours, you have sandy soil; if it is gone in 2 to 4 hours, you are blessed with loam. But if it takes more than 4 hours to drain, you have clay soil. While both very sandy soil and very clay-rich soil are problems for growing tomatoes, sandy soil is generally preferable. Drainage conditions can be improved in both cases by adding peat moss or builder's sand to clay-rich soil and generous amounts of compost to sandy soils.

You also need a level site; a steep slope can cause the water to run off, making the surface of the slope too dry and the bottom, where water collects, too wet. Certainly if water cascades down the slope so heavily that gullies form, the slope is too steep for planting. You can try to terrace the slope to slow down water runoff, but if you have a choice, plant in a more level area.

LAYOUT
Rotation

If at all possible, rotate all your crops (including your tomatoes) to keep soil-borne diseases from the previous year to a minimum. In fact, never plant tomatoes in a spot occupied by any member of the tomato family, such as peppers, potatoes, and eggplants, the previous year. It is true that this is an ideal rule (many gardeners have grown tomatoes in the same spot for 5 or more consecutive years without any trouble), but if you're able to follow it—and most gardeners are—why take chances?

Location

Since tomato plants, particularly when staked, grow taller than most vegetables do, always place them where they won't shade smaller crops. The smallest determinate or nonstaking tomato varieties, however, can be grown in front of many crops. Tomatoes appreciate a bit of shade from taller plants in very hot climates.

GENERAL GARDEN FERTILIZING

Fertilize the garden a few days before setting out your tomatoes. If the soil has been tested, follow directions supplied by your state agricultural agent or other testing service. If not, use compost, rotted manure, or any other organic fertilizer in liberal amounts—a 1-inch to 2-inch-thick layer over the entire area would be fine. These benefit the plants and improve the soil. Or use a commercial fertilizer at the rate specified on the bag. A general all-purpose 5-10-5 commercial fertilizer (5 percent nitrogen, 10 percent phosphorus, and 5 percent potassium) gives good results, but there are many specifically formulated tomato preparations on the market. Generally speaking, the right amount of nitrogen promotes green growth, while phosphorus and potassium contribute to root growth, plant vitality, and healthy flowers and fruit. Avoid fertilizers with a high nitrogen content—they will only stimulate green growth at the expense of fruit. To apply fertilizers, most gardeners spade or till the plot first, broadcast the fertilizer by hand or with a spreader, and then rake the soil two or three times to mix in the fertilizer. Remember not to lime tomato soil unless a soil test shows that liming is necessary.

In the long run, organic fertilizers, such as animal manure and leaves, will improve the soil in the tomato patch, and the results can often be seen within a year. On the other hand, commercial fertilizers can actually harm soil, and if you use too much, you will contaminate the underlying water supply. Long-term overfeeding with commercial fertilizers leads to an accumulation of soluble salts in the soil that causes the locking up of certain nutrients. Another disadvantage with inorganic fertilizers is that weeds thrive on them (and who wants to weed more than

necessary.) Finally, organic matter in the soil is rapidly depleted by overfeeding with chemical fertilizers. One should always be careful to follow directions when applying commercial fertilizers. If you're ever in doubt about how much to use, follow the good, time-honored "half as much, twice as often" rule.

The value of organic matter in the soil is unquestioned. It improves soil "tilth" (texture and workability), increases the water-holding capacity of soils, and through its decay, slowly releases nitrogen and other nutrients for plant use. Organic matter also stimulates root production, maintains the soil-dwelling mycorrhizal fungi that aid plants in the absorption of nutrients, and even reduces soil-dwelling pests, such as root-knot nematodes, by encouraging the growth of parasitic fungi. In addition, carbon dioxide from decaying organic materials helps bring minerals into solution, making them available to plants. Organic fertilizers are of inestimable value to the tomato gardener and a great benefit to the environment and the ecosystem created in one's garden. Try to use them whenever possible. Dig compost, rotted manure, shredded leaves, peat moss into the soil in autumn, incorporate them into planting holes when setting out tomatoes, and top and side dress plants during the growing season. These will never burn plants or leach away during a heavy rain as chemical fertilizers do. Some commonly available organic fertilizers are described in Table 2.1.

Table 2.1: Organic Fertilizers

Average nutrient values of just a few of the many common organic fertilizers (as compared to 5-10-5 commercial fertilizer) are listed below as percentages of nitrogen (N), phosphorous (P), and potassium (K).

Fertilizer	N	P	K	Other nutrients; Comments
Inorganic 5-10-5	5.0	10.0	5.0	May or may not include other nutrients as specified on label.
Alfalfa pellets or meal	2.7	0.6	2.2	Sulfur 0.2%; micronutrients. Breaks down rapidly. Good, all-purpose fertilizer. Available inexpensively in 50 lb. bags as cattle feed.
Bone meal	3.0	2.0	0.5	24% calcium; older references may give much higher NPK values, but modern preparation methods yield approximately this nutrient breakdown.
Blood meal	13.0	2.0	0.0	Rapidly-available nitrogen source. Good for sprinkling on nitrogen-robbing mulches such as wood chips or sawdust.
Compost	1.0	0.5	1.0	0.4% sulfur, 0.2% calcium, 0.1% magnesium, and micronutrients. May contain weed seeds.
Cottonseed meal	6.0	2.0	2.0	May contain pesticide residues.
Cow (steer) manure (dry)	2.0	1.0	2.4	Best composted. May contain weed seeds.
Eggshells	1.2	0.4	0.1	0.4% calcium. Best crushed and composted.
Epsom salts	0.0	0.0	0.0	13.0% sulfur; 10.0% magnesium. Helps plants set fruit.
Fish meal	10.0	4.0	4.0	Rapidly available nitrogen source.
Granite meal	0.0	4.0	0.0	Micronutrients; slow release source of phosphorus.
Greensand	0.0	0.0	7.0	Micronutrients; slow release source of potassium.
Horse manure	2.0	1.0	2.5	1.0% sulfur, 0.2% calcium, micronutrients. May contain weed seeds.
Kelp meal (seaweed)	1.0	0.2	2.0	3.0% sulfur, micronutrients.
Limestone	0.0	0.0	0.0	51.0 to 80.0% calcium, 3.0 to 40.0% magnesium. Used to raise pH.
Oak leaves	0.8	0.4	0.1	Micronutrients. Best shredded.
Poultry manure (dry)	4.0	3.0	1.0	0.2% sulfur, 2.0% calcium; 0.3% magnesium. Best composted, can burn plants when fresh. Great for heating up compost piles.
Rock phosphate	0.0	30.0	0.0	30.0% calcium, micronutrients. Very slow release. Increases pH.
Soybean meal	6.0	1.0	2.0	0.8% magnesium, micronutrients. Rapidly available nitrogen. Available inexpensively in 50 lb. bags as cattle feed.
Sulfur (elemental)	0.0	0.0	0.0	99.5% sulfur, used to lower pH.
Sul-Po-Mag	0.0	0.0	22.0	19.0% sulfur, 10.0% magnesium. Rapidly available source of potassium and magnesium.
Wood ashes	0.0	1.6	5.0	35.0% calcium, micronutrients.

Making Compost

The most useful organic fertilizer is compost. You can purchase it in bags, but there is nothing difficult or mysterious about making it. Composting is simply the disintegration process by which organic materials are broken down by bacteria and fungi. When these break down in a compost pile, they decay more quickly than they would in the soil, yielding the dark, rich, crumbly compost that has so many uses in the garden. A well-made compost has a fertilizer value of approximately 1-1-1.

Almost any plant material can be used to make compost—leaves, grass clippings, vegetable peelings, wood ashes, spoiled hay, even weeds can be composted. Other organic materials you can use in the heap include cornstalks, corncobs, prunings, sawdust, wood chips, pine needles, bark, coffee grounds, and eggshells. Farm- or pet-manure is great if you can get it, but avoid cat and dog manure because they can carry diseases humans can contract. Don't use meat or food scraps with lots of fat; they take a long time to break down and can attract pests.

While many elaborate composting techniques exist, compost can easily be made in about two weeks by following the informal method described here. If you want more complete information, consult a composting manual. If you have enough raw materials, you can make as much compost as your garden requires.

1. Set aside an 8 × 4-foot area in the spring, and fill half the area with a 4-foot to 6-foot-tall pile of shredded leaves, grass clippings, and whatever other organic material you have on hand. To improve the look of your compost pile, you may make a cage of concrete reinforcing wire or a box of four wooden pallets wired together. Or you can purchase a commercial bin. But none are essential to the process.

2. Mix up the material in the pile, and shred it all into small pieces with a rotary mower or shredder. Shredding is not absolutely essential but will speed up disintegration by exposing more surfaces to attack by bacteria and fungi. Unshredded material will take between 4 and 8 months to compost. As you are mixing, sprinkle in some garden soil to add microorganisms, and add enough water to make the shreds feel like a squeezed-out sponge.

3. By the third day, the pile will have begun to heat up. It should be hot enough so that you don't feel comfortable pushing your hand into the center of the pile. If the pile isn't heating up, mix in some green grass clippings or alfalfa pellets to add more nitrogen when you turn the pile the first time.

4. Keep the pile moist, but not soggy, and turn it with a pitchfork or shovel about twice a week. To do this, take the cage (if you are using one), and move it to the other half of

your compost area. Peel off the outside layers of the compost heap first, and deposit them in the center of the empty area. Fork the remains of the pile into the new area. Your compost pile will get smaller as the ingredients in it decompose.

PLANTING
When to Plant
Do not set tomato plants outside until both the air and soil temperatures average at least 60°F over a 24-hour period. The night temperature is just as important as the day temperature. An unprotected plant put out before temperatures rise above 55°F every night will refuse to set fruit. Cold nights are also the most frequent cause of blossom drop in spring.

How to Plant
Whether you grow your own transplants from seed indoors or buy them from a trusted nursery, follow these tips for the actual transplanting of tomato plants into the garden. They will hasten and increase your yield.

Remove Fruits and Blossoms
Prior to setting out plants, remove all their fruits and blossoms. This may seem harsh, but if they are allowed to grow, the plant's root system will never develop properly. Retaining fruits and flowers can only be justified if you value early fruits enough to sacrifice future production.

Timing
Choose an overcast, even drizzly day for transplanting, if you can. It will lessen the chance of transplant shock for the plants. Evening is a good time to set plants, and just before a rain is best of all. Avoid planting on very sunny or windy days. If you must, shelter the plants for several days with HotKaps™, strawberry boxes, paper cones, or similar protection.

Spacing
Tomato plants that you plan to stake should be spaced 2 to 2½ feet apart in rows 3 feet apart. Plants that you plan to let sprawl on hay or another mulch should be planted 3 feet apart in rows 4 to 5 feet apart. Like most instructions, however, these are just guidelines. Standard tomatoes can be planted much closer together, if necessary, and staked plants are often set in sections of 2 × 2 feet, or even 1 × 1 foot, without sacrificing much yield. Vigorous hybrids should be given 2 to 3 feet each way wherever possible. Determinate-type tomatoes, which grow only 2 to 3 feet high in an upright manner, need no more than 1 foot between plants. There is plenty of room for experimenting here.

Preparation
Transplants in peat pots, paper pots, or peat pellets can be set into the planting holes just as they are, with the tops of their containers set at least 1 inch below the soil. Plants in other containers should be removed with as little root disturbance

as possible. To do this, wet the soil thoroughly so the root balls will tip out more easily. Just tap them out by holding the pot upside down and knocking the bottom of the pot with the palm of one hand, while holding the top of the pot with the stem securely between the fingers of your other hand. If your transplants are growing together in a large flat, use a sharp knife to cut out squares of soil, each containing one plant. Be sure to cut down to the bottom of the flat, so that you retain as many roots as possible.

Depth

Dig generous holes several inches deeper than the size of the rootball of each plant. This way you will be burying part of the plant stem; feeder roots form anywhere along a tomato stem, and plants buried deeply will form healthier, denser root systems. They will also be better anchored against possible wind damage.

If your plants are very scrawny and leggy, dig an even deeper hole in the ground to bury more of the stem. The hole should accommodate all but about 3 inches of the leggy plant. Or make a small trench long enough for the stem and lay the leggy plant in it on its side. Very gently bend up three inches of the tip and then cover the remainder of the plant—it will now look as if it has been planted in an upright position. Don't worry about sacrificing any of the indoor growth. The leggy plants will grow better and soon catch up with plants towering above them.

Once the transplants are in their planting holes, press the soil you removed firmly against them, leaving a slight saucerlike depression around each plant to hold water. Be sure to pack the soil tightly against the roots.

Watering

Always water your tomato transplants. Many gardeners feed their young plants at this time with compost tea, or a "booster" of water-soluble fertilizer. Or simply dip the plant roots in the booster solution before planting. Transplants that receive starter solutions are generally more rigorous and mature earlier, and their root systems establish more quickly. There are numerous starter solutions on the market for tomatoes. Usually these solutions are high-analysis fertilizers, such as 6-18-6, all of them high in phosphorous instead of nitrogen and potash. You can make a good starter solution by adding two tablespoons of 5-10-5 fertilizer to a gallon of water. Water each plant with about one pint of this solution after planting.

Cutworm Collars

After setting plants out, make a stiff cardboard or paper collar about 6 inches wide for each plant. You can do this easily by forming a circle with cardboard or paper held in place with a paper clip, or making them from milk containers, open-ended paper cups, or tin cans opened at both ends. Sink the collar into the soil around each plant to about one-half its depth.

Marking

When planting more than one variety of tomatoes, be sure to put identifying markers near each plant so that you know which is which. Commercial plant tags or ice cream bar sticks are good for this. Use a lead pencil or sun-proof marker for writing.

If you don't want to have to deal with the mass of weed seedlings in the background, you'd do well to mulch your tomato bed. This planter's paper will keep weeds in check all season. Spread it over your prepared patch, then cut holes and plant your seedlings right through it.

MULCHING

Covering the soil around your tomato plants with a mulch of almost any organic or any inorganic material not only increases their yield but also affords many other benefits in the garden. For example, mulches reduce the need for watering and weeding by as much as 95 percent. Mulches protect roots against temperature extremes and sudden changes; and, if organic, improve the soil and feed plants. They also protect the soil against compacting by foot traffic; prevent soil erosion on hills; encourage feeder roots in the rich upper layers of soil; prevent plants from being splashed with soil containing disease spores in heavy rains; reduce pollution caused by soil-applied pesticides; produce vital carbon dioxide as they decay; and even stimulate growth in plants by reflecting light to them. Add to this long list of benefits earlier maturity of fruits; larger tomatoes; cleaner, less-damaged tomatoes; and easier harvesting; and it's hard to resist mulching plants in the tomato patch.

Mulching has been nature's way of protecting and providing for plants since time immemorial. The moist, rich, spongy carpet of the forest floor is a perfect example of a mulch. The word *mulch* itself is an ancient one.

There are some minor disadvantages to mulching, but these are easily resolved by choosing the mulch that suits your needs. For example, mulch of any type can contribute to the retention of excessive soil moisture on poorly drained soils in wet seasons. This harms tomato root systems. You can correct drainage problems before you plant or mulch by choosing another site, digging in generous amounts of compost, or building raised beds. Mulches can also provide a hiding place for slugs and mice. To reduce chewing problems, leave several inches of bare soil around the plants' stems.

Mulches

Mulches prevent weed growth and reduce evaporation from the soil. Just about anything that blocks sunlight and other outside elements can be an effective mulch. Organic mulches, such as straw, wood chips, and newspaper, break down over varying amounts of time and enrich the soil. Inorganic mulches, such as plastic sheeting, do not add anything to the soil, but they may be cheap and easy to apply .

No particular mulch is right for each garden or gardener. Several probably will work quite well in your garden, and you must decide which one you want to use, but since organic mulches release soil nutrients as they break down, you should consider these first. Apply very small bits of organic mulches about 2 inches thick; apply very coarse bits of organic mulches as much as 8 inches deep. If weeds break through, the layer was too thin—add several more inches of mulch.

Dry, fibrous, hard-to-break-down mulches such as wood chips or sawdust may pull nitrogen out of the soil and away from plants. To prevent this, dust a high nitrogen fertilizer over the soil before spreading the mulch.

You can mulch plants with just about anything organic or inorganic that isn't toxic to plants. Newspaper, shredded leaves, dried grass clippings, or even chopped weeds are popular and free.

Black plastic, aluminum foil, or weed-barrier landscape fabric are common inorganic mulches you can buy. Every material has advantages and disadvantages, depending on what is available, your growing conditions, the visibility of your patch, and even how much money you care to spend. Table 2.2 lists some commonly used mulches, how to apply them, and their pros and cons.

TO STAKE OR NOT TO STAKE

Bushy determinate tomato varieties—usually the earlier varieties—definitely do not need to be staked and should never be pruned. These stout-stemmed plants grow no taller than three feet in an upright form and stop growing when fruit begins to set. Their upright posture makes staking unnecessary, and if they are pruned, their yield will be considerably reduced.

Semideterminate varieties, which grow a little larger, often don't have to be staked. Indeterminate varieties, tomato plants with stems that grow indefinitely in length and suffer no ills from pruning, are the ones that may or may not need staking. When staking, it doesn't make much difference whether you stake just before or just after setting the plants out. You just don't want to push the stakes through the plant's roots.

Table 2.2: Mulches

Material	Pros and Cons	How to Use
Aluminum Foil	Repels some insects, including aphids, and its reflected light often increases yields. Buy the heavy-duty kind, or look for mylar sheeting, which is much stronger and less prone to tear.	Spread under plants. Weigh down with small stones or anchor the edges with soil.
Asphalt Paper (also known as building or roofing paper)	Forms a long-lasting, if homely, barrier against weeds.	Spread between rows or spread first and cut holes to plant through. Can be covered with a more attractive mulch.
Bagasse (chopped sugar cane residue, sometimes sold as "chicken litter.")	Long-lasting, clean, light-colored, and holds water well.	Apply 2 inches thick.
Bark, Shredded	Lasts a long time, is aesthetically pleasing, adds much humus to the soil, retains moisture, and will not blow away. Large chunks can take a long time to break down and are not the best choice if you till your garden every year.	Apply 2 inches thick.
Black Plastic (polyethylene)	The most popular of the inorganic mulches. It will keep the tomato patch weed-free and fruits clean. Doesn't let rain soak into soil; it has to be picked up and sent to the dump after one season. Inexpensive.	Lay over the soil before tomatoes are planted. Buy plastic at least 1 mil (.0015 mm) thick and spread it over prepared, deeply watered soil on a calm day. Anchor the edges with soil or wire staples about 6 inches long and 1 inch wide—you can make them out of wire coat hangers. Poke small holes all over to let rain water drain into the soil. Cut holes in the plastic and set the transplants in them.
Buckwheat Hulls	Dark, attractive, long-lasting, and do not mat. May blow away when dry.	Apply 3 inches deep.
Old rugs, burlap, old rags, etc.	Good for stubborn, perennial weeds. Old horse-hair or jute carpet pads are great organic mulches, as are old cotton, jute, or wool rugs. Even synthetic ones can be used, but they may	Spread between tomato rows or cut holes and plant through them. Often the underside of a rug is easier on the eyes, so lay them upside down. Can also be covered with a

Material	Pros and Cons	How to Use
	get messy as they start to break down and you'll have to pick up the pieces. Free.	more attractive mulch.
Coconut Fiber (coir fiber)	Long-lasting and attractive.	Apply 2 inches deep.
Compost	Good mulch, but better soil additive. May contain weed seeds, depending on what went into it.	Apply 1 inch thick. Cover with a layer of a coarser mulch.
Corncobs, Ground	Good mulch, but may attract rodents if any corn is left on them.	Apply 2 inches thick.
Corn Stalks	Can either be shredded or used whole. Free.	Apply shredded stalks 2 to 4 inches deep, whole stalks 6 to 8 inches deep and well-stomped down.
Dust Mulch	Shallow cultivation of the soil to create a layer of dust is sometimes used to prevent evaporation from the soil surface. Some experts say all it really does is kill weeds by the act of cultivating. Not the best choice as it promotes soil erosion and does little to improve soil conditions.	Cultivate no more than 1 inch deep once a week or so, or after soil dries after every rain.
Excelsior (wood shaving packing material)	Long-lasting, nonpacking, and free of weed seeds.	Apply 2 inches thick.
Grass Clippings	Dry clippings are a good mulch. Fresh clippings will mat, ferment, and smell if spread thickly. Free.	Apply dry clippings 3 inches deep. Apply fresh clippings no more than 1 inch at a time, and let them dry out before adding additional layers.
Gravel, Marble, and Quartz Chips	Attractive, long-lasting mulch. A ring of sharp gravel around plant stems will prevent mouse damage. Not a good choice in areas you till regularly. Black will help warm soil; white will help keep it cool.	Apply a 1-inch-thick layer over plastic film, asphalt paper, or weed-barrier fabric.
Hay (dried grass and other plants)	Excellent mulch, adds organic matter to the soil. May contain weed seeds.	Apply 6 inches thick after soil is warm.

T a b l e 2 . 2 : M u l c h e s *(continued)*

Material	Pros and Cons	How to Use
Landscape Fabric (weed barrier)	Woven or nonwoven fabric sold to prevent weed penetration. Lasts for many years, and is very tough even if it is walked on. Lets water and air through freely. Not very attractive.	Apply between rows or over entire area before planting. Use scissors to cut planting holes. Cover with a more attractive mulch. Lift and store away from chewing rodents during the winter, and it will last for many years.
Leaf Mold (rotted leaves)	Excellent mulch.	Apply 2 inches deep.
Leaves	Shred leaves to prevent them from blowing about or packing down into a waterproof layer. Free. You can shred leaves by running a rotary lawn mower back and forth over them.	Wet down and apply 1 to 2 inches thick.
Mushroom Soil	Rich in organic mater, usually weed-free. Very fine, and may crust in dry conditions.	Apply 2 inches deep.
Newspaper	Newspapers break down and feed the soil. They also suppress weeds. Bare newspapers can be unattractive, and can blow around if not anchored. Free. Shredded or pelletized newspapers are also good mulches.	Apply at least 6 to 8 sheets thick, overlapping edges. Anchor with rocks, or cover with a few inches of any organic mulch. Apply shredded or pelletized newspaper 2 inches thick and wet down.
Peanut Hulls	Excellent mulch. Can blow around and may attract rodents if any peanuts remain.	Apply 2 to 4 inches thick, depending on how coarse the bits are.
Peat Moss	Not a good mulch because it dries out, crusts, and resists rewetting.	Work into soil to add organic mater instead.
Pine Needles	Attractive and useful. Use them if you have them, and they need to be cleaned up off pavement areas. May be overharvested from wild areas.	Apply 2 inches thick.
Plastic Film (Polyethylene)	Black is the most common color (see Black Plastic), but other colors can also be used. Clear is not a very good choice since weeds can thrive under it.	Same as for Black Plastic above. Clear plastic is good for prewarming soil in the early spring. Replace with black plastic just before planting.
Salt-Marsh Hay	Good mulch. Free of weed seeds. Slow to break down, so it lasts longer than some organic mulches, but it doesn't feed the soil as fast either.	Apply 4 to 6 inches deep.

Material	Pros and Cons	How to Use
Sawdust	Sawdust or shavings are a good mulch. Avoid black walnut though. Compost it first.	Apply 2 to 4 inches deep, depending on how fine or coarse it is.
Seaweed	Seaweed that washes up on the beach is a superb mineral-rich, growth-promoting, weed-free mulch. You may want to hose it off first away from the garden to reduce the amount of salt clinging to it.	Apply 2 to 4 inches deep.
Straw (the dry stems of harvested grain such as wheat or oats)	Coarser than hay, but more durable. Straw may contain a few grains of the crop and an occasional weed seed.	Apply 4 inches thick, shaking and fluffing the straw to make a loose, uniform mulch. Four-inch slabs of bales laid close together, or even entire rectangular bales, make a good smothering mulch for stubborn perennial weeds.
Rocks, Stones, and Concrete Chunks.	If you've got them, why not put them to work? They smother weeds, and absorb the sun's warmth, slowly releasing it into the soil.	Spread a solid ring of rocks starting a $1/2$ inch from the stem and extending at least 5 inches out. Flat rocks weighing a few pounds each are the easiest to work with but just about any rock can be used. Fit them together as close as possible.
Water	In recent USDA experiments, sturdy, clear plastic bags filled with water and spread around tomato plants increased yields by 20%. The water absorbs the sun's warmth, slowly releasing it into the soil, and can help extend your season for weeks in both spring and fall.	Use a hose to fill clear plastic bags spread around plants with water, and close them securely. Make sure there are no sharp twigs or rocks under them. Plastic gallon jugs filled with water and packed closely together would also work and are free.
Weeds	Weeds that haven't gone to seed can be used as a mulch. Free.	Let weeds dry slightly so they won't reroot, or spread them on top of a layer of newspaper.
Wood Chips	Wood chips are a good, long-lasting mulch, but aren't the best choice for areas that you till regularly. Sometimes you can get tree trimmers to deliver them for free. Better for shrubs and perennials.	Apply 4 inches thick.
Wool	Waste wool mats are sold for mulching plants. They are a long-lasting, organic mulch.	Spread around plants.

Whether or not to stake tomatoes is a difficult question to answer because both ways offer benefits. Unstaked plants that sprawl naturally may yield more fruits—perhaps 20 tomatoes compared with about 12. Another benefit of unstaked plants is that the fruit they produce is generally less "sunscalded." The fruit tends to crack less, and there is less likelihood of blossom-end rot in most seasons. They are less susceptible to the ravages of drought, and they are easier to protect during the cold weather toward the end of the growing season. Finally, fewer plants are required for the same total production and not staking involves less work.

On the other hand, tomato plants that are staked always fruit and ripen somewhat earlier than unstaked ones, though not much. Staking also results in fruit that is cleaner, free of ground spots, less subject to rotting and slug damage, and slightly larger on average than fruit from unstaked plants. Perhaps the most important reasons for staking are that the fruits are easier to spot on the vine and are easier to pick, the garden looks neater, and staked plants are easier to walk around. Finally, gardeners with limited space can grow nearly twice as many staked as unstaked plants in the same size space.

A final note on staking plants: The new ring-culture tomato-staking methods described later in this chapter will produce significantly more fruit than letting plants go unstaked.

Letting Plants Sprawl

Should you elect to let your vigorous indeterminate tomato plants sprawl naturally, try to give each plant at least 15 square feet of room. Space the plants 4 to 5 feet apart in rows that are also 4 to 5 feet apart. But don't neglect the plants just because they are sprawling. Examine them periodically for slug and hornworm damage, and apply corrective measures where and when needed. In addition, try to give the fruits something to rest on so that they don't develop ground rot and blemishes. For this, use an organic or nonorganic mulch, or make a low platform from cinder blocks and long sticks or pallets over the bed and let the plants grow naturally over the slats.

An extravagantly fruiting plant in a square cage.

SUPPORTING OR STAKING PLANTS

You are really only limited by your own ingenuity when it comes to choosing supports, if you elect to stake or otherwise support your plants. Listed below are some commonly used possibilities and tips on how to best use them.

Wooden Stakes

By far the most common tomato-support system, stakes are made of cheap lumber, usually 1 inch × 1 inch boards, 5 feet long, but 6- or 8-foot stakes are even better. You can push, hammer, or dig the wooden stakes about one foot into the soil at a distance of 3 to 5 inches from the stems of the tomato plants. The underground portion tends to rot out every year or two, but you can use what's left until the stakes become too short. You can also use scrap lumber and straight tree branches for stakes.

Bamboo

Bamboo poles thinner than 1 inch in diameter are the least effective stakes you can buy because they can't support healthy tomato plants. Select only those with diameters 1 inch or more.

Multiple Wooden Stakes

When growing heavy-vined tomato varieties, some gardeners sink a ladderlike structure next to each plant made of 2 wooden stakes with foot-long cross supports nailed to the main stakes at 2-foot intervals. In a similar fashion, you can make a boxlike support system for each plant from four stakes and cross supports. Multiple staking systems like these enable you to tie vigorous varieties in more places.

Wire Fences

You can make a sturdy fence for tomatoes by stretching heavy wire mesh, wide enough to reach through, between stout 8-foot-high stakes. Set the stakes 10 feet apart and drive them 2 feet into the ground.

Double Wire Fences

You can plant a row of tomatoes between a row of two wire fences, as described above, set 1 to 2 feet apart. This eliminates some tying up of tomato plants.

Other Fences

Any standing metal or wooden fence that is at least 5 feet tall makes a good support for tomato vines.

Wire Cages

Wire cages are great for holding up tomato plants because they allow plants to develop naturally, providing shade for ripening fruit and reducing sunscald and cracking. And plants set inside them don't need pruning or tying. You can also easily fit wire cages with plastic to provide protection for plants in cold weather. You

A wire cage made from sturdy wire mesh, like the one supporting this 'Celebrity' tomato, cuts down on tying chores and makes it easy to harvest luscious fruits.

can buy sturdy wire cages or make your own from lengths of sturdy, 5-foot-wide concrete reinforcing wire. The openings in this type of wire are large enough so you can reach through, yet it is quite sturdy. Using an ordinary pair of pliers, cut and join the wire into a cage or cylinder 5 feet high and 2 feet to 5 feet in diameter. Place a cage over a single plant and press the bottom edge of the cage firmly into the soil. A few short stakes woven through the mesh and pushed into the soil will help keep a top-heavy cage upright. Do not use the inexpensive ones sold at many local discount stores; the weight of the plants will tip them over before mid-summer.

Japanese Rings

A cage-staking method pioneered by Japanese and English gardeners, the Japanese ring-staking system is really an improvement on the preceding wire-cage method and could help a single plant to produce up to 100 pounds of fruit. With this system, the plants are grown outside a wire cage that is filled with nutrient-rich, organic matter. To set up the system, place a wire cage made from concrete-reinforcing wire firmly in the garden. Line this cage with a 2-foot-high strip of screening or burlap secured in place with clothes pins. Fill the screen-lined cage with a 2-foot-high mound of layered material. Follow this with 6-inch layers of organic material or compost and rich loamy top soil. Scoop out the top of the mound into a shallow saucer shape that will hold water. Set 4 plants in the ground around the perimeter of the cage and, as they grow, tie them to the wire cage with a soft cloth. Keep the soil in the center of the ring moist, and add fertilizer to it every 2 to 3 weeks. Eventually, the plants will grow over the wire and even flop down into the ring.

Wooden Teepees or Tripods

This system is especially good for vigorous tomato varieties. To set it up, space three 7-foot-long poles or relatively straight branches about two feet apart in a circle. Hammer the poles about a foot into the ground, and pull them together at the top. Tie the tops together with stout cord or wire—the structure will resemble a teepee. Plant one plant in the center of the circle and prune it to a single stem. Place a six-foot wooden stake in the ground next to it. When the plant's main stem grows to the top of the stake, tie it to the teepee top. Tie all side branches to the three teepee poles.

Trellises

You can buy already made trellises or make your own from lumber or tree branches. When making your own, use stronger wood for the vertical supports than for the horizontal supports. Make the trellis at least 6 feet high and as long as needed. Place the horizontal supports about 1 foot apart.

Pea Trellising

With this method, you use string to support tomatoes as you would to support pea plants. Set heavy 8-foot-tall posts in the row about 10 feet apart and stretch a length of heavy wire across the top from post to post. Tie heavy cords to the wire. The cords should be long enough to drape down to the plants. Attach each cord to the stem of a plant just above the ground. As the plant grows, keep it pruned to a single stem and twisted around the cord.

Sunflowers

You can use sunflowers as living tomato stakes. To do this, plant sunflowers near the tomato plants when you set them out. Set 3-foot high wooden stakes next to the tomatoes too, and let the tomatoes climb the stakes at first. When the tomato plants reach the top of the stakes, the sunflowers will be ready to use as natural stakes for the rest of the season. Tie the tomato stems

to the sunflower stalk with soft cloth ties. Fertilize and water heavily to provide for the needs of both plants. Besides acting as natural stakes, the sunflowers will shade the tomato plants and help prevent sun-scalded fruit.

Tomato Stake Extensions

Gardeners often underestimate how tall tomato plants will grow and they often end up with vines that grow much taller than their stakes and frequently break at the top when loaded with fruit. It's easy to solve the problem. Simply add bamboo or wood extensions to the original stakes. Overlap the bamboo or wood extension against the original stake by at least 1 foot and fasten it to the stake with 3 pieces of tightly twisted wire or strapping tape.

Tying Plants to Supports

Tying up tomato plants requires some care. For example, you should never bend tomato vines at sharp angles when tying them because they snap very easily. Don't tie anything too tightly around the stem itself, or the tie may "cut off the circulation" of the stem as the plant grows. Secure the tie tightly around the stake at a point that corresponds to 2 to 3 inches above a leaf stem on the tomato; loop the tie loosely around the main tomato stem below the leaf stem, and fasten it with a square knot. You should be able to slip your finger inside the tie loop with the stem after it is tied. Try to keep any flower clusters pointed away from the stakes; otherwise the tomatoes may be crowded between the stem and the stake as they enlarge and become injured or mis-shapen as a result. Check plants once a week and tie up any stems that need support. Use soft twine, strips of coarse cloth, lengths of old nylon stockings, or raffia for ties.

PRUNING

Some gardeners choose to prune the large, rambling tomato varieties, but pruning is not necessary. The main advantage of pruning vigorous plants is that they are easier to stake so they can yield earlier fruit. It is best to prune moderately, if you prune at all. The quality of fruit on pruned vines can be inferior to that on unpruned vines because when the leaves are removed, plants do not produce as much sugar and starch. Plants in tight spaces, however, or indoors, may need more severe pruning to stay in their assigned spaces. In very humid climates or during rainy periods, a light pruning may help prevent disease problems by opening up the plant to air and sunlight.

Should you decide to prune your plants, you have many options. Whichever method you select, however, you should use your fingers, a technique called "pinching," to do the pruning itself. Just grasp the small shoot you want to remove with your thumb and forefinger and bend it sharply to one side until it snaps. Then pull the shoot off in the opposite direction—this will prevent injury to the leaf axil or main stem. If you use a knife or hand pruner, it is a good idea to disinfect the blade with rubbing alcohol between touching plants to avoid spreading diseases from one plant to another.

Single-Stem Pruning

Single-stem pruning yields fruit one to two weeks before other methods do. To do this, remove all side branches or suckers that appear, leaving only the main stem (with its flower blossoms) to grow. Check plants for suckers once a week and remove them while they are just forming; this can be done at anytime without harming the plants, even when the suckers are more than one foot long. Take care not to disturb the fruit buds that appear just above or below the points where leaves are attached to the leaf stem. Also, remove any lower leaves that turn yellow or brown, snapping them off flush with the stem. If you want to limit the growth of the plant to the height of the stake, pinch off the top of the plant when it reaches the top of the stake.

Multiple-Stem Pruning

This method allows two or more main stems to develop. It will produce more fruit than single-stem pruning and gives more protection against sunscald. The technique is almost identical to single-stem pruning except that you leave one or more suckers near the base of the main stem and allow them to grow into an additional main stem.

Modified Single-Stem Pruning

Some gardeners claim a 3-fold increase in fruit production by allowing all side branches and suckers to develop until they form their first blossom cluster. Then the suckers are pruned off directly above the flower cluster. The suckers are then tied to the stake. This method is easiest to use on single-stem plants, but you can also use it on multiple-stem plants.

WATERING

Tomatoes are composed primarily of water, and like most vegetables, need a constant supply of water to thrive. Tomatoes need one to three inches of water per week from rainfall or other means. This amount will vary somewhat depending on heat, wind, humidity, and the condition of your soil. For example, plants will need more water on hot, dry, and/or windy days and less on cool, humid, and/or calm days. As for soil condition, if the soil is very sandy, the plants may need more water than if they were planted in a water-retentive loamy or clay-rich soil.

Where All the Water Goes

To understand why plants need so much water, think about where rain or irrigation goes after it lands on the ground. Some water may run off across the surface of the ground, out of reach of your plants. Some water sinks down into the ground and finds its way into the ground-water reserves, out of reach of plant roots. The remainder of the water is retained by the soil, much as a sponge retains water, where the plant roots can absorb it as needed. Over time, however, some of the water held in the soil evaporates, unless the plant has been mulched to help prevent this loss.

Gardeners know that plants drink up a great deal of water from the soil. What you may not know is that a great deal of water is "breathed out" from tiny pores in the leaves when the plants transpire. Only a very small amount of water is used to make stems, leaves, and fruit.

WISE WATERING

As a thrifty gardener, you can do many things to reduce the amount of water that runs off, drains out of reach of the roots, or evaporates from the surface of the soil. Follow these tips to get the most out of your water.

Improve the Soil

Working compost, well-rotted manure, or rotted leaves into any type of soil helps it retain more water. Growing and turning under a green manure also adds water-holding organic matter.

Mulch

Mulching your plants can reduce the amount of water that evaporates from the surface of the soil. It can also keep the surface of the soil soft and ready to soak up rain or irrigation water, preventing it from running away over the surface of the soil.

Keep Soil Moist

Strive to keep the soil moist but not soggy at all times. It should feel like a well wrung-out sponge. Moist soil lets plants take all the water they need, whenever they need it, but doesn't drown them by forcing all the air out of the soil.

Plant Drought-Resistant Varieties

If water is hard to come by in your locality, or your summers are hot and dry, try planting drought-resistant tomato varieties.

Water Regularly and Frequently

Light, frequent watering is fine if the soil stays moist so it can soak up every precious drop, but detrimental to the plants if you let the soil dry out between watering. Light, infrequent watering tempts the roots to the surface where they then dry out and die. Water deeply if you can't keep the soil moist.

At any rate, do not wait until your plants are wilting or the soil is dusty-dry to water them. Fluctuating dry and wet spells can stunt tomato plants and cause blossom-end rot and cracked fruits. It is better to give plants a drink a few times a week than to drown them with the same amount of water once a week.

Inch-by-Inch Method

Keeping a rain gauge in your yard is a good way to keep track of how much water nature has provided for your plants, and it will help you estimate when your plants are likely to need a drink. A rain gauge can be as simple as a coffee can with a ruler for measuring how much rain has fallen.

To figure out how much water you should give your plants, subtract the amount of rain (in inches) you've gotten over the last few days from the appropriate amount given below. Multiply the result by the number of days since you last watered, and subtract the amount of rain received in the same days to get how much you need to add.

If the temperature is under 70°F and humid, start with 0.10 inches per day.

If the temperature is under 70°F and dry, start with 0.15 inches per day.

If the temperature is 70°F to 80°F and humid, start with 0.20 inches per day.

If the temperature is 70°F to 80°F and dry, start with 0.25 inches per day.

If the temperature is 80°F to 100°F and humid, start with 0.30 inches per day.

If the temperature is 80°F to 100°F and dry, start with 0.35 inches per day.

If the temperature is over 100°F and humid, start with 0.40 inches per day.

If the temperature is over 100°F and dry, start with 0.45 inches per day.

You will need to adjust this advice to fit your individual situation, but it will give you a good place from which to start. Use the "squeeze" method below to make your final decision. You will get a feel for your plants' needs as the season progresses.

One inch of water is equal to about 55 gallons of water per every 100 square feet of growing area. (Multiply length by width to get square feet.) You can determine how much water your hose puts out by timing how long it takes to fill a 5-gallon bucket. Commercial drip systems usually are rated by gallons per certain number of feet per hour.

Squeeze Method

Feeling the soil under the mulch around your tomato plants is the best method for ultimately deciding if your plants need water. You can use it exclusively or use it after you estimate with the inch-by-inch method described above. Soil should feel moist, like a squeezed-out sponge. If it feels dry, it needs water—no matter how much rain or water has been added lately. If it feels wet or sticky, it needs no water—no matter what any other calculations may suggest.

The best time to water is in the early morning, especially if you are using a watering method that wets the leaves so that the leaves have a chance of drying during the day. When tomato leaves are wet for more than 3 hours, they become very susceptible to leaf-blighting or leaf-spotting fungi. Don't compound these problems, which occur naturally with long rains, by using the garden hose carelessly.

If you want to spring for a handy gadget, an electronic, moisture-sensing monitor gives you a reading on the moisture in the soil by remote buried sensors. The sensors feed back information to the control unit, which automatically waters when the soil needs it. You needn't lift a finger. Timers that water a certain amount every day are also available and are less expensive than garden computers. They are fine in areas where the weather is consistent. They are, unfortunately, useless in areas where it rains heavily 1 week and not at all the next.

How to Water

In most cases, the best watering methods are those that keep the leaves dry, put the water on the soil, and only add it as fast as it can soak in. A few watering methods are outlined below.

By Hand

The old, reliable watering can and garden hose are still fine watering methods. They require more time and effort on your part, but are relatively inexpensive. Even empty plastic gallon jugs are useful watering tools (premeasured, too!). Just be sure to direct the water under the plants, not on top of them, for best results.

Hoses tend to deliver the water a bit too fast. To reduce the speed and allow the water to seep slowly and deeply into the soil, tie an old sock around the nozzle, and lay it next to a plant. Turn the water on low and let it gently soak the plants for a few hours.

Sprinklers

While they are easy to use, conventional sprinklers are not, as a rule, the best choice. They get the leaves wet, and it is usually difficult to water a large area evenly—some plants get plenty, while others get less. In very hot, dry conditions, sprinklers can be useful for cooling plants in the heat of the day (assuming you have plenty of water). In terms of water conservation, sprinklers are the least practical means of watering.

If you choose to use a sprinkler, adjust it so that water doesn't run off the patch. You can also set 4 or 5 coffee cans around the tomato patch to help you measure how much water you've added, as well as to determine if all the areas are getting about the same amount of water.

Drip Irrigation

This is a simple, ancient, and very effective way of watering. Gardeners long ago discovered that sinking an unglazed, slightly porous pot beside a plant leaked the water out to the plant over a long period of time. You can do the same thing next to each plant by sinking a large can with a few holes punched in the bottom and watering into these cans. A plastic gallon jug with a small hole in the bottom makes a good, portable drip watering tool.

Drip irrigation systems are efficient, but expensive, variations of drip watering. They involve putting together sections of hose with built-in "emitters" or "drippers," or plugging individual "emitters" into solid hoses just where you want them. Some systems also use adjustable-output "micro sprinklers" that water a single plant. Kits are available at your local garden center or by mail order, and aren't very hard to install. Drip systems can be used for container plants, too. Once you've arranged the system and covered it with mulch, it is a simple matter of turning it on for a set amount of time. Drip systems limit the water pressure that reaches the emitters, so run off is rarely a problem.

Soaker Hose

Soaker hoses with small holes in them are the simplest improvement on the single plant methods. The leaky pipe types are better than those that actually spray water. Just snake them around under the mulch and turn them on for as long as you need to every few days. Again, make sure you adjust the water pressure so water doesn't run off over the surface.

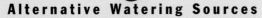

Alternative Watering Sources

The rain barrel, not exactly a modern water-saving device, is coming into its own again. Rain barrels, painted to match either house, trim, or shingles, are best set under gutters to catch runoff from the roof. The drain downspout is placed inside the barrel, which should be covered to discourage mosquitoes. The water collected can either be ladled out later, or the barrel can be fitted snugly with a pipe and tap at the bottom. The barrel is often rigged near the top with a pipe connection and hose so that overflow from heavy rains will flow into a second barrel or off to an area where it can seep into the soil.

You can also save and use cooking, wash, rinse, and bathing water (small amounts of soap and detergent will do tomato plants no harm.) Some areas have regulations concerning how you can use this so-called "gray water," which you would do well to follow. Other areas have no regulations.

Apply gray water directly to the soil, under mulch, to prevent any germs that may be in it from splashing onto the fruit. You'll need to filter it if you plan to use it with a commercial drip system as bits of dirt, food, or fuzz could clog up the drippers.

WEEDING

Weeds are only uncultivated plants growing where they are not wanted, but they do, nonetheless, cause billions of dollars of damage on farms every year. Weeds remain with us despite the dollars spent each year to destroy them, and weeds will always be with us, if only because of their obstinacy: Weed seeds buried in a bottle on the Michigan State University campus in 1890 were found to be viable a century later!

Weeds definitely compete with tomatoes—as they do with all vegetables—for moisture, nutrients, and light. They also harbor insects and diseases that can attack tomatoes. Harmless-looking chickweed, for example, can host the virus known as "spotted wilt," which will infect tomato plants if an insect feeds first on the chickweed and then on the tomato. Ironically, the better your soil, the more weeds you'll have. But all weeds can be easily handled with a little effort.

Mulching can practically eliminate weeding chores before they start, and the next best way to beat weeds is hand-pulling and cultivating. After a rain or deep watering is the best time to remove weeds by hand. Or cut them off anytime about one inch below the soil surface with a sharp hoe, weed knife, or cultivator. Take care not to disturb the tomato plant's roots or to turn up new weed seeds from deeper down in the soil. Weeds can go right into the compost heap so long as they contain no ripe seeds.

Some gardeners like to keep the soil around their plants tilled up. This will keep weeds at bay. Loosen the soil no deeper than one inch so you won't damage the roots of the tomato plants.

Herbicides are not recommended in the tomato patch, as tomatoes are quite susceptible to herbicide damage. Black plastic, or any other mulch, will keep the weeds down, and won't take any more time to spread than you would spend applying herbicide. Mulches—organic or inorganic—are far safer for you and the environment. If you choose to use an herbicide be very careful to keep it off your plants, and always apply according to the directions on the label.

FERTILIZING

Tomato fertilizing can be a relatively simple matter. A tomato plant will yield (and often yield well) if it is just set in prefertilized ground and watered regularly. However, this isn't always the case, and tomato yield will invariably increase if plants are given more attention.

If you have prefertilized the ground where your tomatoes are planted, and fed the transplants with a starter solution as described earlier, you won't need to fertilize again until the first fruits appear on the plants. In fact, wait until these fruits are as big as half dollars for best results. Choose one of the following methods.

Liquid Fertilizer

Feed plants with any of the many liquid tomato fertilizers on the market. These are applied as per directions on the container with a watering can,

sprayer, or hose feeder. To make 1 gallon of a less-expensive liquid fertilizer from a dry 5-10-5 fertilizer, tie up 4 ounces of the 5-10-5 in a piece of cloth. Swish this around in 1 gallon of water for a few minutes, then leave the cloth in the water for 2 days. When you remove the cloth bag, the material remaining will only be the crushed rock used for the fertilizer binder. Water plants every 10 days with this solution, 1 gallon per plant. Note that this solution is much cheaper, but it will not supply as many nutrients to your plants as a carefully formulated commercial preparation.

Compost Tea

Water plants with compost tea, which is made by soaking compost in water, or a diluted liquid fish fertilizer—both good organic options—once a week.

Dry Fertilizer

Scatter one heaping teaspoon of 5-10-5 fertilizer around each plant and mix it into the top $1/2$ of soil 8 to 10 inches from the stem. Repeat this procedure once or twice a month.

Controlled-Release Fertilizer

Use a single-application, controlled-release fertilizer that provides nutrients slowly over the course of the season as directed on the bag.

Compost

Spread one spadeful of compost around each plant once or twice a month.

Table 2.3: Solutions for Common Nutrient Imbalances

Problem	Symptoms	Treatment
Nitrogen Deficiency	Stunted, slow-growing plants, leaves turning light green or yellow, starting with older leaves. Flower buds yellowing and dropping off.	Feed with a fertilizer high in nitrogen such as blood meal.
Nitrogen Excess	Overabundance of lush, vibrant green leaves, few blossoms or blossoms that look normal but drop off without setting fruits (and weather is warm).	Pinch off some of the excess leaves. Do not feed the plants high nitrogen fertilizers. Let weeds grow near plants and pull them when they are 1 foot high to soak up extra nitrogen. Plants will grow out of the problem.
Phosphorus Deficiency	Leaves turn purplish beginning with the undersides. Leaves small, stems slender. Fruiting delayed. Often seen in seedlings in cool soil.	Spray seedlings with seaweed extract. As soil warms up, the problem should resolve itself. Enrich soil with rock phosphate or any fertilizer high in phosphorus.
Potassium Deficiency	Older leaves yellow with green veins, then turn bronze. Slow, stunted growth. Young leaves crinkled. Few fruits—those that do appear, are soft and ripen unevenly.	Add wood ashes or other potassium-rich fertilizer to soil. Mulching also helps.
Calcium Deficiency	Young leaves pale and flabby, growing tips die. Plants stunted	Correct pH and mulch to maintain soil moisture. Add limestone, bonemeal, or crushed egg shells.
Boron Deficiency	Abnormally bushy plants with black areas at the growing points. Shoots wither and die. Fruit with dark or dry areas.	Water plants with a solution of 1 ounce borax (in the laundry section of your supermarket) dissolved in 25 gallons of water).
Manganese Deficiency	Slow-growing, stunted plants. Leaves light-green turning to yellow (dead spots appear in the yellow and spread). Few blossoms and little or no fruit.	Water plants with a solution 1 ounce of epsom salts (ask your pharmacist) dissolved in 25 gallons of water.
Iron Deficiency	Young leaves pale green or yellow with green veins.	Spray plants with chelated iron or seaweed extract.
Zinc Deficiency	Young leaves narrow and yellowing. Plants stunted, older leaves bluish-green. Few or no flowers.	Spray or water plants with seaweed extract.

Green Manure Cover Crops

Another way to build up the tomato patch soil organically is to grow "green manure" cover crops. To do this, sow the garden toward the end of the growing season with red clover, vetch, annual grass seed, rye, buckwheat, oats, or millet. Fertilize the cover crop when it comes up and dig it under the following spring. Legumes, like red clover and vetch, are the most valuable cover crop, and add the largest quantities of nitrogen to the soil. All of the above green manure crops are good soil conditioners. Their roots will also loosen heavy soils and help hold the particles of sandy soils together.

HARVESTING

Tomatoes taste best and are most nutritious when eaten "dead-ripe," that is, straight from the vine. The peak of ripeness usually comes about 6 days after the first color shows. Tomatoes will stay in this dead-ripe condition on the vines only 2 to 3 days before beginning to decay, so you must keep a sharp lookout in the garden for ripening fruits. Dead-ripe fruits are strong in color (for example, bright red or orange), full, and shiny. If you've never pulled a tomato straight off the vine and eaten it in all its sun-warmed glory, you're in for a real treat!

Storing Ripe Tomatoes

Almost any variety of tomato will keep for a few days to one week in a cool place after they are harvested at the peak of ripeness. Do not try to store blotched ripe tomatoes; instead, use them immediately or they will rot quickly. And don't put ripe tomatoes in the refrigerator. Refrigeration destroys their flavor. (Cut or cracked tomatoes can be put in the refrigerator to prevent them from spoiling if you can't use them immediately.)

Several tomato varieties keep much longer than average when picked ripe and are excellent for storing. Burpee's 'Long Keeper,' for example, stays fresh in storage for 6 to 12 weeks or longer and tastes better than the average winter supermarket tomato you can buy. Try starting a few plants later than usual (count back from your average first fall frost date to find out when) and harvesting the ripe fruits the latest possible date before storing them. Spread the fruits out so they are not touching each other. Some gardeners wrap tomatoes individually in newspaper.

Ripening Green Tomatoes
While it would be nice if every fruit could ripen on the vine, in most North American climates this is not a realistic hope.

Storage tomatoes like these 'Long-Keeper' fruits will last for weeks if kept in trays or wrapped in papers so they don't touch each other.

Plant ahead for fall eating with a variety that stores well, such as these 'Long-Keeper' tomatoes.

You can help tomatoes to ripen on the vine late in the season by using one of the many protection measures described in Chapter 5. You can also try a technique called "defoliation." Once green tomatoes have reached their mature size, remove most of the leaves on the plant. This pruning procedure often hastens ripening of tomatoes by 5 or 6 days. However, defoliating the plants exposes them to frost damage, so be sure to protect them if frost threatens.

Old-timers say that the best way to hasten the ripening of tomatoes after a few on the vine have reached full size is to grasp the main stem at ground level and pull upward until the roots snap. The largest fruit on the plant will ripen faster. The plant, which will only wilt a bit, will quickly recover with no permanent damage. Try this on only 1 or 2 plants until you get the hang of it. It's a good trick to know, if only to help you get the first tomato in the neighborhood in late spring or early summer and to ripen tomatoes before frost kills them in the fall.

If you are faced with green fruit at the end of the season, don't despair. Green tomatoes can be cooked in a variety of ways, and full-size, partially ripe or even green tomatoes can be picked and ripened in several ways. Leaving a few inches of stem on each tomato when harvesting the fruits from the vine seems to help them ripen. Green tomatoes can be disinfected with a solution of 1 teaspoon of household bleach to 1 quart of water. Dry them thoroughly before storing. Sometimes green tomatoes stored for ripening taste better if they are scalded with hot water and their skin peeled off just before they are eaten.

Try one of the following ripening methods:

- Harvest full-size, blemish-free, green tomatoes and ripen them indoors. Contrary to popular belief, light has little effect on ripening tomatoes. Putting green tomatoes in a bright window, for example, will not hasten ripening. But temperature does effect ripening—tomatoes don't ripen well at temperatures below 65°F or above 85°F. Tomatoes kept above 65°F will ripen in 2 to 3 weeks.

- To stretch out the ripening period, you can store green tomatoes wrapped in newspaper or spread out on a shelf at a temperature of 55°F. They will ripen a bit slower than those kept at room temperature and they'll last longer.

- Pull up an entire tomato vine with green fruits attached and hang it upside down any place where the temperature is always between 55°F and 75°F, such as a basement, attic, garage, or spare room. The fruits will continue ripening long after the plant has wilted.

Chapter 3

Plant Portraits

Tomatoes come in more shapes, colors, and sizes than most people can imagine—including yellow, white, green (when ripe), and striped varieties. In 1994, seed suppliers in North America offered almost 650 different tomato varieties in their catalogs, and each year the U.S. Department of Agriculture tests another 2,000 new varieties. The tomatoes range in size from the tiniest patio types to huge, 3 pound-plus beefsteaks. Their shapes are round, ribbed, elongated, even square, so that the slices fit neatly into sandwiches. There's also a hollow tomato variety for stuffing.

A bountiful harvest of fresh tomatoes

There are also many "antique," or heirloom, varieties that date back to the 19th and early 20th century, before hybridization led to today's disease-resistant cultivars. Many seed companies specialize in heirloom varieties and promote these historical seeds. There are also many private seed savers dedicated to saving these endangered varieties.

If you buy plants from your local nursery or garden center, your choices will probably be limited to a few of the most common hybrid and standard tomato varieties. This may be just fine for your purposes. But if you really want to explore the full range of the tomato kingdom, you will need to grow your own plants from seed. Starting your own plants is one of the great joys of tomato gardening. While you'll need to provide the right germination conditions for the seeds, growing plants from seeds is not tremendously difficult. You'll find complete instructions in Chapter 4.

TIPS ON CHOOSING THE RIGHT VARIETY

Following are some tips for getting the best tomato for your money:

1. Always buy your seeds from a reputable company. If you can find a company that grows its own seed in a climate similar to your own, so much the better. Leftover tomato seeds can be used in subsequent years provided they are well-sealed and stored in a dark, cool place. They may last up to 4 years, but you would be better off using fresh seeds each year.

2. Height and bushiness of the plant are serious considerations, particularly for gardeners growing tomatoes in small spaces.

3. Other factors to consider in selecting seeds include taste, size, shape, color, mildness

(acidity or nonacidity), disease resistance, and cracking resistance. Homegrowers need not consider whether the variety has "firm skin" or "uniform ripening" characteristics as these belong to the "good shipping" types and concern primarily commercial growers.

'Roma'

4. Your intended use for the tomato may dictate your selection. For instance, if you want to use your tomato crop for preserving or for making tomato paste, you'll want to select a variety that has a strong tomato flavor and lasts a long time in the refrigerator. 'Roma' is a good variety for making tomato paste.

5. Disease-resistance may be of special interest to you if a particular disease is prevalent in your area.

6. You may be concerned about the "days to maturity" (the time it takes for a transplant to bear ripe fruit) if the growing season is short where you live.

7. Finally, your priority may be in choosing a unique tomato plant, a novelty no one else in the neighborhood grows.

In the lists that follow, you'll find a selection of the best and most unusual tomato varieties. Keep in mind that no tomato variety will be all things to all people. Varieties are bred with particular traits in mind and usually excel in those. The best approach is to try 3 or 4 varieties listed in this chapter, choosing at least one plant each

of the early, mid-season, and late-ripening varieties in order to have fresh tomatoes throughout the entire growing season. You could even have a supply of winter tomatoes if you plant "keepers," which you'll learn about in Chapter 5.

THE MOST DELICIOUS TOMATOES

Since taste is a purely subjective matter, you'll have to experiment to find the tomato you think tastes best. Tomato flavor depends, to a large extent, on the ratio of sugar to acid in the tomato. If the ratio is low, the fruit will be sour or have an insipid taste. Most experts say that the fleshier tomatoes have a higher ratio of sugar to acid, and tomatoes with greater percentages of jelly and seeds will have a lower sugar/acid ratio. But many people prefer a tomato packed with seeds, and for this reason grow large-fruited varieties with 5 to 10 seed chambers. One thing we know for sure: Everyone loves home-grown, vine-ripened tomatoes.

SUPERBIG TOMATOES

In 1986, home gardener Gordon Graham of Edmond, Oklahoma, grew the biggest tomato ever recorded in the *Guiness Book of World Records*: a whopping 7-pound, 12-ounce tomato of the 'Delicious' variety. The year before, Gordon Graham grew the biggest American tomato plant ever, measuring 53 feet, 6 inches tall. While no one should expect to beat Graham's record the first time out, tomato plants can yield inordinately large fruits when properly grown. If you want to grow some big tomatoes, start with one of the varieties listed below. Most will weigh over three pounds and have a large enough diameter so that a single slice makes a sandwich layer.

'Abraham Lincoln'
'Beefsteak'
'Burgess Jumbo Hybrid'
'Burpee Big Boy'
'Burpee Supersteak Hybrid'
'Climbing Trip-L-Crop'
'Colossal'
'Crimson Cushion'
'Delicious'
'Garden Peach'
'Giant Belgian'

'Giant Oxheart'
'Golden Boy'
'Golden Oxheart'
'Jumbo'
'Ponderosa'
'Ponder-Heart'
'Supersonic'
'Supersteak'
'Ultra Boy'
'Watermelon Beefsteak'
'Winsall'
'Wonderboy'

'Supersteak Hybrid'

'Delicious'

'Big Beef Hybrid'
'Boatman Miracle Climber'
'Climbing Trip-L-Crop'
'Giant Tree'
'Jung's Giant Climber'
'Oxheart'
'Ponderosa'
'Trellis 22'
'Vineripe'
'Winsall'

PROLIFIC TOMATO PLANTS

According to the *Guinness Book of World Records*, a single tomato plant grown at the Tsukuba Science Expo Center in Japan in 1988 produced 16,897 tomatoes, making it the most prolific tomato-producing plant of all time. Unfortunately, the variety name of this prodigious producer was not recorded. A number of tomato plants actually grow more than 20 feet high when trained against a building, and several gardeners claim to have harvested 250 tomatoes from a single vine. There is documentation of a sprawling, staked California plant that "covered a space of eight feet square" and yielded 170 pounds of fruit. Many of the tomatoes in the preceding list of Superbig Tomatoes are capable of such heavy fruiting, with proper watering and fertilizing, but those in the following list are the best plants for gardeners interested in the biggest harvest of tomatoes.

EXTRA-NUTRITIOUS TOMATOES

Tomatoes have the distinction of being known as "the oranges of the vegetable garden" because of their high vitamin C content. They are also rich in vitamins A, B1, and B2, and low in calories, containing only about 4 calories per ounce. It is interesting to note that, according to studies made at Michigan State University's Department of Food Science, home-grown tomatoes ripened on the vine have 33 percent more vitamin C than their commercially grown, artificially ripened counterparts.

Some tomato varieties are especially nutritious. These include 'Burpee's Jubilee;' 'Caro Rich;' 'Doublerich;' and many of the oranges, yellows, blues, and pinks described later in this chapter. 'Doublerich,' which was developed by crossing garden types with a tiny, wild Peruvian tomato, has twice the vitamin C of most tomatoes. 'Caro

Rich,' a flavorful orange type, is 10 times richer in vitamin A than ordinary varieties due to the surplus of beta-carotene in its orange pigment. One 'Caro Rich' tomato provides up to 2 times an adult's minimum daily requirement of vitamin A and is rich in vitamin C as well.

'Big Beef'

UNUSUALLY COLORED TOMATOES
Most Brilliant Red Tomato
If you want to grow the most brilliant red tomato, try 'Crimson,' a variety developed from a native Philippine species by scientists at the University of Toronto. 'Crimson' is said to be two or three times the color intensity of common red types.

Orange, Yellow, and Tangerine Tomatoes
Yellow tomatoes have more sugar than their red counterparts, and consequently taste less acidic. Favorites include 'Caro Rich,' 'Husky Gold Hybrid,' 'Lemon Boy Hybrid,' 'Yellow Pear,' 'Jubilee,' 'Golden Boy,' and 'Golden Ponderosa.'

'Lemon Boy'

Pink or "Blue" Tomatoes
Some recommended pink tomatoes are 'Brandywine,' 'Giant Belgium,' 'Dutchman,' 'Early Detroit,' 'Gulf State Market,' 'Oxheart,' 'Pink Delight,' 'Pink Ponderosa,' 'Watermelon Beefsteak,' and 'Winsall.' "Blue" is a designation sometimes given to pink tomatoes when they have a purplish-pink color.

White Tomatoes

Like orange- and pink-fruited types, white fruits are relatively sweet. They have a pale color, very close to white-skinned when ripe, and their ripe flesh looks almost paper white. Some good choices include 'Snowball,' 'White Wonder,' and 'White Potato Leaf.'

Green Tomatoes

All tomatoes are green before they ripen, but a few varieties are green when fully ripe. Perhaps this detracts from their taste if, as gastronomes tell us, the eye and taste buds work in tandem. Yet green tomatoes are surely a conversation piece, or something for winning a bet ("I'll bet you that this tomato is perfectly ripe!"). Look for the variety 'Evergreen.'

Striped Tomatoes

Tomatoes with distinct stripes are probably the ultimate in tomato novelties. Two varieties include 'Tiger Tom,' which has attractive stripes in red and orange-yellow, and 'Tigerella,' which has a red skin with golden stripes.

ODD-SHAPED TOMATOES

Some tomatoes refuse to conform to shape and others are bred to be unusual. Whichever the case, they are interesting. 'Pink Ponderosa' is an old favorite that often sets grotesquely shaped fruits (to the conformist's eye, anyway), and

'Beefsteak,' an old-fashioned ribbed tomato, also offer a striking contrast to today's uniformly round varieties. 'Liberty Bell,' a Bicentennial-year introduction, is actually shaped like a bell pepper; 'Sausage,' too, is appropriately named; and 'Square Tomato,' like several paste types, is almost square in form (good for sandwiches!). Try some of the odd-shaped, small-fruited varieties, such as egg tomatoes, and red or yellow pears.

Little 'Yellow Pear' tomatoes are delightfully sweet and colorful in salads.

HUSK TOMATOES

These tomato cousins are not literally tomatoes, but worth a mention here. The sweet, tangy fruits of husk tomatoes come packaged in papery skins or husks. Hawaii's renowned 'Poha Jam' is made from one type of husk tomatoes. Another type, known as "tomatillo," is used to make authentic salsas and other Southwestern dishes.

'New Yorker'   *'Viva Italia Hybrid'*

Close cousins of tomatoes, these easy-to-grow tomatillos add an authentic touch to Southwestern salsas.

STAKELESS TOMATOES

Bushy, determinate tomato varieties (as opposed to sprawling, indeterminate types) do not need to be staked in the garden because they grow no more than 3 feet tall in an upright form and will stop growing when fruit begins to set. Some of the better nonstaking types include:

'Bonanza'
'Celebrity'
'Fireball'
'Galaxy'
'Husky'
'Gold Hybrid'
'New Yorker'
'Rocket'
'Roma'
'Stakeless'
'Viva Italia Hybrid'

TOMATOES CHOSEN FOR THEIR BEAUTY

Many varieties of tomatoes can look good in the flower or vegetable garden and serve as edging plants, such as the diminutive 'Tiny Tim,' only 1 foot or so tall, and other midget varieties. Other varieties provide interesting foliage for the garden, like the variety 'Abraham Lincoln,' for example, that has bronze-colored leaves that stand out in the flower garden. Plants with interesting leaf shapes are always welcome in the garden, and for that you might try 'Giant Italian Tree,' which sports enormous, potato-shaped leaves.

TOMATOES FOR SPECIAL AREAS

- **Drought-resistant tomato:** Try 'Porter,' 'Red Cloud,' 'Hotset,' 'Summerset,' and 'Pink Ideal' for gardens that are difficult to water.

- **Heat-resistant tomato:** 'Heatwave' hybrids set fruit in unshaded locations during the most intense summer heat, while most other tomatoes won't set fruit at temperatures above 90°F.

- **Keeper or rot-resistant tomato:** 'Burpee's Long Keeper' stays fresh up to 12 weeks or more in winter storage after the tomato season is over. 'Golden Treasure' and 'Thessaloniki' also store well.

- **Paste tomato:** 'Roma' is recommended for making tomato pastes.

- **Sandy-soil tomato:** The variety, 'Starfire,' performs well in sandy soil.

- **Stuffing tomato:** 'Liberty Bell' and 'Ruffled' are "hollow" tomatoes excellent for stuffing.

- **Wet-area tomato:** 'Pearl Harbor' is especially good for low, damp grounds.

- **Wine tomato:** 'Giant Belgium' is recommended for making old-fashioned tomato wine.

DISEASE-RESISTANT TOMATOES

Today most tomatoes are bred for disease tolerance, or resistance. For example, the letter "V" next to a tomato variety's name in a seed catalog, on a seed packet, or on a plant marker means resistance to verticillium wilt. "F" stands for fusarium wilt resistance; "N" stands for nematode resistance; and "T" stands for mosaic virus resistance.

THE EARLIEST TOMATOES

Early tomatoes bear fruit in about 43 to 63 days from the time plants are set outside. Their quality is excellent, though usually the fruit is smaller than main-crop varieties. There are far more determinate (bushy) or semideterminate plants, which do not require staking, among the early varieties. Burpee's new 'Northern Exposure' is an excellent choice. There are hundreds more in the catalogs of seed companies, including 'Burpee's Early Hybrid,' 'Manitoba,' 'Maritimer,' 'Paul Bunyan,' 'Rocket,' 'Spring Giant Hybrid,' 'Starfire,' 'Sunset,' and 'Tom Tom.' Cherry tomato types that bear early

'Heatwave'

include 'Tumbler Hybrid,' 'Gardener's Delight,' 'Small Fry,' 'Johnny Jump-up,' 'Tiny Tim,' and 'Window Box.'

'Burpee's Big Boy Hybrid'   'Burpee's Jubilee'

'Good & Early'   'Gardener's Delight'

'Delicious'
'Lemon Boy Hybrid'
'Long Keeper'
'Marglobe'

MAIN-SEASON TOMATOES

Main-season tomatoes, by far the most numerous of all varieties, bear in 66 to 80 days from the time plants are set out. They are large, indeterminate (tall-growing) plants that bear the large fruits, exceeded in size only by the late-season types. Some of the best include:

'Abraham Lincoln'
'Ace'
'Better Boy Hybrid'
'Big Beef Hybrid'
'Burpee's Big Boy Hybrid'
'Burpee's Big Girl'
'Burpee's Jubilee'
'Burpee's Heatwave Hybrid'
'Burpee's VF Hybrid'
'Caro Rich'
'Celebrity Hybrid'

'Marglobe'

'Rutgers'

'Marion'
'Perfecta'
'Rutgers'
'Stakeless'
'Supersonic'
'Tropic'
'Ultra Boy'
'Vine Ripe'
'Whopper'

LATE-SEASON TOMATOES
These varieties bear the largest fruits of all and yield fruit in about 80 to 100 days from transplanting. All are large, indeterminate (tall-growing) plants. They are difficult to grow in sections of the country with short growing seasons. These varieties include:

'Beefmaster Hybrid'
'Beefsteak'
'Big Crop Climbing'
'Big Red'
'Boatman'
'Brimmer'
'Burpee's Supersteak Hybrid'

'Supersteak Hybrid'

'Climbing Trip-L-Crop'
'Colossal'
'Crimson Giant'
'Giant Belgium'
'Giant Italian Tree'

'Honey Field Tomato'
'Jung's Giant Climber'
'Lakeland Climbing Tomato'
'Manalucie'
'Manapal'
'Miracle Climbing Tomato'
'Oh Boy!'
'Oxheart'
'Pink Ponderosa'
'Pink-skinned Jumbo'
'Ponder-Heart'
'Rampo'
'Rockingham'
'Tropic-Gro'
'Winsall'

ALL-AMERICAN TOMATOES

Keep your eyes open for 'All-American Selection' (AAS). These are varieties that have performed well in field trials across the country run by the All-America Selection committee of the American Nurseryman's Association and awarded gold, silver, and bronze medals as excellent plants for all America to grow. 'Burpee's Big Beef Hybrid,' 'Celebrity Hybrid,' and 'Husky Gold Hybrid' are recent winners.

WHERE TO OBTAIN SEEDS

Seed companies often offer different varieties from year to year, adding new ones and dropping old ones. If you cannot obtain one of the varieties mentioned in these pages from your favorite seed catalog or local nursery, consult a garden seed directory, such as *Gardening By Mail, The Garden Seed Inventory* (Seed Saver Publications), or *Cornucopia* (Kampong Publications). Such directories list varieties by name and give the names and addresses of seed companies offering them at the time of publication.

Chapter 4

Starting Tomato Plants from Seed

Growing your own tomato plants from seed provides you with the widest range of options for varieties to grow and gives you the opportunity to grow your plants your own way, particularly if you want to grow them organically. You can time your planting so you will have seedlings exactly when you want them—whether for early planting or for mid-summer planting in the case of long-keeping tomatoes—rather than when they happen to appear at the corner store.

SOILS FOR GROWING TOMATO SEEDS

Tomato seeds will germinate in almost any soil, or even in none at all. Some gardeners germinate seeds on moist paper towels sealed in plastic bags kept in a warm (80°F to 90°F) place, and carefully plant the sprouted seeds in a seed-starting medium after a few days. But to grow tomato seedlings, you must select the soil you use carefully. Soil from the garden may be inexpensive, but it is too heavy to use to grow healthy seedlings. Garden soil mixed with equal parts of coarse builder's sand and peat moss (or leaf mold) makes a serviceable seed-starting medium. Other mixtures for growing seedlings are 1 part peat moss to 2 parts sand, or 1 part compost to 1 part sand and 2 parts soil. When you use soil, you are taking the chance of bringing in diseases or other problems with the soil. It is far better, though more expensive, to use a commercial soil mix as a medium for starting tomato seedlings. These sterile mediums are free of disease-producing organisms and weed seeds.

Vermiculite

Vermiculite is a lightweight, expanded-mineral product—that is, mica that has been heated at 1,800°F until it breaks and puffs into tiny fluffy pieces. A completely sterile substance containing magnesium and potassium, vermiculite holds and releases large quantities of both minerals and water for plant growth. Another advantage in using vermiculite is the ease with which tomato seedlings can be lifted from it without any damage to their roots. However, vermiculite doesn't have the body to hold up large seedlings. In other words, it's perfect for starting seeds, but not satisfactory for growing plants until they're set out in the garden. It is also devoid of nutrients, except for minerals, and seedlings grown in it have to be fed weekly with a liquid plant food after they grow about one inch tall. Otherwise, they must be transplanted to a more nutritious soil mixture. If you use vermiculite, use only horticultural grades, not insulation grades.

Blended Synthetic Soil Mixtures

These are the best and most-developed mixtures for starting tomato seeds and are highly recommended. Blended synthetic soil mixtures are composed of peat moss, vermiculite, and various fertilizers. All you have to do is toss one or more bags into a pail, add water, and stir until the mix is damp (not wet). Not only is this medium lightweight and free of disease, insects, and weed seeds but it is also dense enough to hold large seedlings and is supplemented with plant nutrients. Seedlings can be lifted out of flats easily for transplanting into individual pots. What's more, the same kind of mixture can be used for the repotting job. Some good brands are Burpee Tomato Formula, Burpee Seed-Starting Formula, Jiffy Mix, and Pro-Mix. All come with instructions.

Chilling Tomato Seedlings

Research suggests that tomato seedlings that are chilled as soon as they have their first true leaves bear earlier and yield more fruit. Various studies made at Michigan State University show plants chilled at this time will bear earlier and heavier yields of fruit because the flowering process is stimulated. Chilled plants grow stockier and thicker stems, enabling them to survive transplanting better. Though chilling is not essential, it is an exception to the traditionally higher temperatures required for growing tomato seedlings and interesting to note.

One way to chill plants is to move the flats to a cooler room in the house. The plants must, of course, have light while they are being chilled. The seedlings are best chilled at 50°F to 55°F for two weeks. Afterwards, continue growing them at temperatures of about 70°F during the day and 65°F at night.

CONTAINERS FOR STARTING SEED

You can start tomato plants in anything from store-bought, self-watering, seed starter trays to homemade flats. Such containers include old milk containers, cake pans, clay pots, aluminum trays, paper cups, plastic bottles—any container that can hold soil and hold its shape when wet will do. Make certain the container you use is clean. Wash it out with a solution composed of 10 parts water and 1 part household chlorine bleach before using it. Always make drainage holes in containers, and cover the drainage holes with a sheet of paper towel to prevent dirt from clogging them. Seedlings should only remain a few weeks in such flats before being transplanted to peat pots or other larger containers. Many gardeners start seeds right in individual peat pots or 6-pack type, seed-starting flats, both of which eliminate the need to pot seedlings up in individual pots later. If you have plenty of space, go with individual cells or pots.

Seed-starting supplies and young plants

PLANTING SEEDS

Now that you've selected the tomato varieties, soil mixtures, and containers you like best, and decided when you need to start them, you're ready to plant your tomato seeds. Follow these steps for successful seedlings:

1. Soak the seeds in a mixture of water-soluble fertilizer for 2 hours before drying and planting them. Recent tests prove that plants grown from fertilizer-soaked seeds are invariably heavier-rooted and healthier.

2. Fill your container(s) to within ½ inch of the rim with an artificial soil mix.

3. Thoroughly water the soil mixture in container(s) before seeding. This can be done by setting them in a sink or dishpan with a few inches of water in it.

4. Estimate how many plants you'll need, and plant twice as many seeds so that you'll have a good choice of plants when thinning later. If planting in individual containers, plant 2 seeds in each.

5. Sprinkle seeds on the surface of the planting medium, spacing them about 1 inch apart in all directions, and sift a scant ¼-inch-thick layer of planting medium or vermiculite over them. You can also poke each individual planting with the eraser on a pencil, which is about ¼ long, drop 1 seed in each, and cover it with a pinch of planting medium.

6. Water gently with a fine spray or with a tin can with a dozen or so small nail holes punched in the bottom. If you water too heavily, you may wash out the seeds.

7. Tomato seeds don't need light to sprout, but they do need moisture. Slip the moist seed flat into a "tent" made with a clear plastic bag to keep the soil from drying out. Tie it up loosely. If the soil does appear dry, however, water it gently again. You can also use a pane of glass or a layer of newspaper to cover the seed flat. Whenever excess condensation (some is normal) appears on the plastic or glass, pull the covering back a little to allow the moisture to evaporate. Open the end of the bag once the seeds germinate, but leave it in place until seedlings are ready to be transplanted to a larger pot.

Kord Fiber Pack

8. Seeds also need warmth to germinate. Until the seeds germinate, they should be kept at a temperature of 75° to 85°F. Keep them any place where that temperature is maintained until they germinate—for instance, on top of the refrigerator.

9. Tomato seeds germinate in 7 to 10 days. Once seedlings emerge, they need strong light and cooler (65°F to 70°F) temperatures.

TIMING

Tomato seedlings should be about 7 to 8 weeks old when you plant them out in the garden. You can easily determine local planting times by calling your state agricultural extension service or consulting experienced local gardeners. Count backward from that date to find out when to plant most of your tomato seeds. If you plan to put some plants out before that and use season-extending devices to coddle them until they can survive unprotected, plant seeds for those plants about four weeks earlier. Figure when to plant seeds of the "keeper" variety tomatoes by counting back the number of days to maturity from the average first fall frost date. Unless you have plenty of space and plenty of big pots, don't be tempted to push planting dates in the hopes of getting bigger plants. Remember, the object is to grow healthy, stocky plants, not stunted, root-bound ones. A small, healthy plant will eventually out-produce a larger, stunted one.

THINNING TOMATO SEEDLINGS

The first leaves to appear when the young plants break out from the soil aren't true leaves, but cotyledons, or "seed leaves," which are filled with starch to nourish the developing plant. As soon as the seedlings show their first "true" leaves (shaped like mature tomato plant leaves) and are 1 to 1½ inches high, they should be thinned. Thinning allows the remaining plants more room to grow and greatly improves their quality. As much as you'll hate to do it, snip off every second plant (no matter how good it looks) at ground level with a pair of scissors.

LIGHT REQUIREMENTS

Tomato seedlings need roughly 12 hours of light a day, so it is important to keep them in the sunniest, southernmost window in the house or provide fluorescent grow lamps for them—otherwise they'll become long and spindly, reaching for the light. Light and temperature being equal, a bathroom window is preferable to a window in the usually dry air of a living room because tomato seedlings like humidity. A kitchen window, no matter how warm and sunny, can be a fatal place to grow tomatoes. If there is the slightest gas leak in the kitchen, the sensitive tomato will detect it. The slightest concentration of gas, too small to be detected chemically, will affect tomato leaves. In fact, florists were said to use potted tomato plants as early indicators of gas seeping into their greenhouses. Remember to turn the plants every day—otherwise they'll grow toward the sun and develop a permanent lean. If you don't have a warm sunny window in the house, you could either make do with as much sun as you have (and risk weak, leggy plants), or use artificial lighting.

Many types of grow-lamps and fixtures are available, ranging in price from $10 to hundreds of dollars. Some are available on stands—others are fixtures to hang from the ceiling. Wide-spectrum fluorescents make particularly effective grow lamps. Two 4-watt tubes suspended over a table will provide a complete light source for seedlings, even in a windowless basement. Adjust the height of the light every few days to keep it about 1 inch above the topmost leaves, or place the seedling plants on a stack of newspapers, and remove layers as necessary to keep the leaves at the proper distance from the lights. You might consider buying an inexpensive timer to turn the lights on and off.

TIPS FOR FERTILIZING AND WATERING SEEDLINGS

Tomato seedlings shouldn't need any additional fertilizing when a prefertilized soil mixture is used. But if their leaves begin yellowing, apply a liquid fertilizer at half strength. If you don't use a prefertilized soil mix, or use a sterile planting medium like vermiculite, feed tomato seedlings weekly with a diluted liquid fertilizer high in phosphorus and potash, but low in nitrogen. You can also use compost. Remember not to apply too much nitrogen because it can harm tomato seedlings, making them tall and leggy.

Keep the planting medium moist, but never soggy. Water very carefully from the top, keeping the water off the seedlings themselves or soak the container(s) in a pan of water until the planting mix is sufficiently moistened. Keep in mind not to let the soil get too wet because it may create damping-off, a fungal condition in which seedling stems rot at the soil line and the seedlings flop over and die.

THE IMPORTANCE OF TRANSPLANTING SEEDLINGS

(If you started your seedlings in individual pots, you don't need to read this section.) Tomato seedlings can be planted directly into the garden from flats, but it is not recommended. Experts agree that tomatoes should ideally be transplanted at least once while still indoors. Tomato seedlings seem to like the less-cramped root conditions in a new, larger container. Some gardeners transplant tomato seedlings from flats to 2-inch pots when they are 2 inches tall, then again into a larger pot when they reach about 4 inches. It won't matter whether you transplant your seedlings once or twice indoors, but plants raised without any transplantings tend to be weaker and more spindly than those that have been transplanted.

To avoid transmitting any diseases, be sure that your hands are clean when you transplant tomato seedlings. Be particularly mindful of the effects that tobacco has on sensitive tomato plants. Tobacco mosaic, a deadly plant disease, can be carried to the plant from nearby smoke. If you smoke, don't do it while handling tomato seedlings.

Follow these simple steps for transplanting seedlings:

1. To avoid plants suffering any setback from transplant shock, use peat pots for the transplanting pots. These biodegradable containers, available at all garden centers and from seedsmen, can later be planted whole in the garden without removing the young plants and disturbing their roots. Made of wood pulp and ground peat moss, with soluble fertilizer sometimes added, peat pots must be filled with sterilized potting soil before your seedlings are planted in them. (Remember, however, when you do plant them outside, to be careful to bury the entire pot. Any part of a peat pot sticking

out of the soil acts as a wick pulling moisture away from plant roots.) A 3-inch pot is good for standard variety tomato seedlings and a 4-inch pot is good for hybrids. (Tests by Burpee show that hybrid tomato seedlings in 4-inch pots produce earlier and yield more heavily than those raised in smaller pots.)

Peat pots with young seedlings

2. Fill the peat pot with a new batch of the same planting medium used for the seed flat. Growers often fill their pots with a

slightly richer mix of compost, sand, and soil in equal parts at this stage, but any planting medium will do.

3. After watering the 4-inch-tall seedlings carefully, remove them one at a time from the seed flat. A flat stick, a spoon, or even an apple corer can be used here, but the best tool is probably a dull knife. Cut each plant out with a block of soil so that its roots are intact—then plant each seedling in its individual peat pot. Hold the transplants by the rootball or the leaves, never by the stem, because even the slightest pressure can break a tomato seedling's stem.

4. Keep the transplanted seedlings in the same sunny window (or under lights) and at the same temperatures as before. Fertilize and water in the same way, taking care never to let the soil dry out.

HARDENING OFF

When your plants are 7 to 8 weeks old, and about 8 inches to 12 inches tall, they're ready for transplanting outside. Prepare your plants for the outdoors by hardening them off, a process that gradually accustoms the plans to the outdoor conditions, toughening the tender tissues that they developed indoors and reducing injury from unexpected temperature drops. Set them outdoors for increasing amounts of time each day for about 7 to 10 days prior to transplanting,

and cut back on watering. It's best to put the plants outside in a protected place, such as against the house or a garden wall on days that are not too cold or windy. Bring the plants in each night. Do this gradually—½ hour the first day, slightly longer the second day, until they are outdoors almost the entire day. You can also transfer the plants to a cold frame to harden them off, which is more convenient if you aren't able to move them in and out every day. (See Chapter 5 for tips on cold frame construction.) Giving the plants less water slows down growth and enables them to better withstand the shock of transplanting to the garden.

"How Many Plants Will I Need?"

In most cases, a tomato plant will bear from 12 to 20 fruits, or 8 to 10 pounds of fruit. Tomatoes easily yield 80 portions per 10 feet of row. Generally speaking, 2 plants per person would be sufficient for a family, but how many plants you need will depend on such factors as how sunny your yard is (tomatoes yield less when not in full sun); whether you intend to do any canning; and, of course, how many tomatoes you want to eat. If you want to can tomatoes for a year's supply, figure on growing as many tomatoes as you can reasonably can, about 10 plants per person.

Chapter 5

Extending Your Tomato Season

With a little extra planning, you can have fresh tomatoes on the table 4 to 6 weeks before most gardeners have them in the summer, 4 to 6 weeks after most gardeners have them in the fall, and even during the winter. The methods for growing tomatoes in this chapter outline not only how to extend your growing season by growing the right varieties at the right time, but also how to grow plants indoors and in greenhouses in winter.

Remember, when using any of these methods, observe the same rules previously given regarding seeds, soils, containers, and seedling care.

GROWING EARLY TOMATOES IN THE GARDEN

Growing early and late tomatoes is a gamble. Some years you'll have excellent results and other years may be disappointing. The first step to success with early and late tomatoes is to start with the right seeds. Choose tomato seed of an early-bearing determinate (bushy) variety. Follow the steps outlined in this chapter for best results with varieties.

'Early Girl'

Steps to Success

Begin by sowing your seeds inside three to four weeks earlier than you normally would. Plant the seeds in individual pots and tend them like any tomato seedlings, especially in regard to chilling and hardening off the plants as previously described in Chapter 4.

When selecting a site to plant early tomatoes, take advantage of the warm microclimatic conditions in your yard. Even though your zone is generally the zone listed on the USDA Hardiness map, changes in the topography of your property, protection from winds, southern and western light, and reflected heat and light will all influence the climate and make an area warmer by as much as 5 degrees. Choose one of the warmer microclimates for your early tomatoes, and put a thermometer in the garden so that you know exactly the temperatures.

Prewarm the soil where you plan to plant for at least 2 weeks before planting day by pulling back any organic mulch and covering the bare soil with a sheet of clear plastic held down around the edges with soil or boards.

Set the hardened-off plants out in the prewarmed planting area three to four weeks earlier than usual. Observe all outdoor transplanting tips noted in Chapter 2.

Protection from the Cold

All early tomato transplants need protection from cold and frost. This can be provided in a number of ways with individual plant covers made of glass, plastic, grocery bags, or even tin. Use one of the following protective covers described below or improvise a method of your own.

Cloches. For centuries, gardeners have used cloches (bell-shaped glass covers) to protect plants from the cold. Hotkaps™, the cloche's modern equivalent, are inexpensive, miniature hothouses made of weather-resistant wax paper that protect plants against the elements. They should be kept on the plants at night and removed during the day if the weather warrants it. Follow the manufacturer's directions for best results.

Paper bags. You can also use large paper grocery bags to protect early plants. Slip the bag over the tomato stake and weight the bottom of it with stones or soil to keep out cold air. Use the paper bags whenever excessive sun, frost, or winds threaten the young, tender plants. Pull them up on the stakes when the weather is good.

Plastic containers. Gallon-size plastic containers provide excellent protection for early plants. To make these miniature greenhouses, simply cut out the bottoms of the containers. As with the other protective covers, remove them when the weather warms up.

Tin cans. Large-size tin cans—the bigger the better—afford excellent plant protection if both tops and bottoms are cut out and the top hole is covered with a small pane of glass or clear plastic.

Water tubes. Wall o' Water™ plant protectors store heat in their water tubes during the day, and release it slowly all night, making them very effective for protecting early planted seedlings.

Storm-windows greenhouse. If you're handy, you can build a makeshift "greenhouse" for a row of early tomato plants from old storm windows. Stand the windows lengthwise and dig the storm windows about 8 inches into the soil on all sides of the row. Seal each space where the windows join with tape, and top the greenhouse with more storm windows or clear plastic.

Wood and plastic greenhouse. Similar to the storm-window greenhouse above, this makeshift greenhouse uses a simple wooden frame and a clear plastic covering.

Wire and plastic tent. You can also make a plastic tent "greenhouse" by draping clear plastic over tall wire wickets placed in a row, clipping the plastic to the top of each wicket with clothespins, and holding the plastic in place at ground level by covering it with soil.

Wire and plastic cylinders. Tall, open-top cylindrical cages made of concrete reinforcing wire can be placed over each early transplant and covered with clear plastic for protection. Later you can remove the plastic from the top and sides, leaving the cylindrical cages to support your plants.

Bushel baskets. Bushel baskets covered with clear plastic make good protectors.

Bales of hay. Bales of hay placed in a square around a plant or two and topped with clear plastic or a large pane of glass are good, too.

In very cold weather, you may also want to drape a blanket over any of the sturdier plant protectors mentioned above for extra warmth. All coverings must provide adequate ventilation for early plants, and this is particularly important in areas where cold or cool spring weather is occasionally broken by high temperatures. Tight coverings can suffocate plants on such days. It's a good idea to provide small openings in the covering to let excess heat escape on warm spring days (making sure the holes can be sealed when it gets really cold), or go into the garden on unseasonably warm days and remove all coverings, replacing them again each night.

Another way to protect tomatoes planted early outside from frost is to spray your plants. During a frost, a light sprinkling of water for a couple of hours in the morning will sometimes prevent plant tissues from freezing. According to Cornell University botanists, you should apply 1.10 inches of water an hour just as soon as the temperature falls near 32°F, and continue sprinkling the plants at least once a minute until the ice is gone.

Tomatoes will not set fruit when night temperatures are below 59°F, but hormone sprays can help the plants set fruits 2 to 3 weeks earlier if used on plants set out in cold weather. Flowers will also fall off when there is little sunlight. Hormone sprays prevent the cutting-off, or abscission, layer from forming between the bud and stem. The abscission layer causes the flower to drop before the fruit is set. The hormone spray makes the fruit set and holds it on the plant. Plants treated with hormone sprays will also produce more—sometimes twice as many—fruits that are larger and meatier. In fact, treated fruits will be seedless, a blessing to those who like beefsteak tomatoes. Hormone sprays are inexpensive and widely available; Blossom-set™ and Duraset™ are two good ones. Carefully follow all directions and spray into the openings of the flowers. Incorrect use of hormone sprays or application when an excess of nitrogen has been used to fertilize plants may cause premature softening of tomatoes, puffiness, or large hollow spaces in the fruit.

GROWING EARLY TOMATOES IN A COLD FRAME

A simple cold frame that will meet the needs of most amateur gardeners can be made with cheap lumber and ordinary storm windows or an old glass door. First, measure the storm window you have and buy or collect enough 2 × 8 second-grade wood to enclose it. Then measure off and

An automatic self-venting cold frame is a handy tool for any tomato enthusiast, especially one who can't hang around all day watching the weather. This portable model functions in and around your garden throughout the year.

enclose with string a rectangle in a spot facing south on high ground where the cold frame can stand permanently. Be sure that the soil has good drainage; if it doesn't, dig out the bottom soil and replace it with coarse rock and gravel before refilling the frame. For soil in any cold frame with good drainage, dig out about one foot of earth from the top of the string-enclosed area and refill the space with 6 inches of rich, light soil. Place the 4 boards for the frame against the sides of the excavation. The tops of all the boards should be exactly the same height above the ground—about 2 inches—and must be level. Finally, butt the boards together at right angles, nail them together solidly with 3-inch-long

nails, and top them with the storm window. With 6 inches of soil removed from the enclosure, plus 2 inches on top, this cold frame will give your plants 8 inches worth of headroom to grow in, but if a taller frame is desired, simply use wider boards. I've often used several 2 × 12-inch boards. If you want a wider cold frame, use 2 storm windows, or more, and additional lumber—there's no limit to how big the structure can be. The trick in the whole operation is to make sure all your measurements are exact so that the structure is airtight when you place the storm window on top. Do not treat the wood with chemical preservatives; even inexpensive woods will last several few years before needing replacement. Many gardeners build cold frames, as above, and use heavy-grade, clear plastic sheeting as a cover in place of glass, anchoring the plastic with boards so that it isn't blown away and pulling it back when ventilation is needed. Others substitute concrete blocks or bricks for the wood used in building the structure. For additional reflected light and heat, the inside walls of frames are often coated with white or silver paint.

Equip your cold frame with a thermometer on the inside. When temperatures drop very low, back soil, hay, or sawdust up against the outside of the frame and cover the glass with a quilt, blankets, mats, straw, black plastic, or similar insulating material. When the weather is hot (above 70°F) during the day, prop the front end of the storm window up on bricks to provide ventilation for the plants. You can also shade the cold frame during unusually hot weather. Water plants in the morning so they dry off by night. When seeding tomatoes directly into a cold frame, use only seeds treated against damping-off fungus. As an added precaution, sterilize the soil by pouring 5 or 6 gallons of boiling water over it one or more days before planting. Sow the tomato seed about 1/4 inch deep, following the same procedures as for seeds planted directly into the soil outside. Water carefully, taking care not to get the soil too wet, when the temperature is low or on cloudy days. If you are growing the plants in place and don't intend to transplant them to the garden, remove the glass entirely

when average day and night temperatures reach 70°F. The plants can then grow as high as you like. Fertilize and cultivate as you would for any tomato plant growing outside.

SEEDING EARLY TOMATOES INTO A HOTBED

A hotbed is little more than a heated cold frame. Many gardeners used to use fresh horse manure to generate the heat inside the cold frame, but today most rely on the relatively inexpensive electric soil-heating cables available. A 3 × 6-foot hotbed will need approximately 40 feet of a cable rated at about 200 watts. Build the hotbed the same way as a cold frame, but add an 1/8-inch board below ground level. Arrange the cable on the bottom of the hole, and spread a 2-inch bed of vermiculite over it. Cover that with 1 inch of soil. Then place a piece of wire mesh over the dirt to protect the cable from accidental damage, and cover this with 6 more inches of soil mixed with compost, or 2 cups of a complete fertilizer such as 5-10-5.

Tomato seeds can be sown in hotbeds even earlier than in cold frames, a full eight weeks before the average last frost in your area. Sow seeds just as for a cold frame, and care for the plants in the same manner. Be particularly careful about ventilation in a hotbed, though. About 2 weeks before setting your plants out in the garden, turn off the heat in the bed, using it as a cold frame from that point on and gradually hardening off the plants.

GROWING LATE TOMATOES OUTDOORS

You can easily stretch the outdoor tomato season many weeks beyond the first fall frost date in your locality by using the same techniques described for early tomatoes. Just how long the plants will bear depends on the severity of the weather, but the use of heavy plastic and other protective devices will certainly insure tomato production long after gardeners nearby have pulled out their plants. Always cover late-season tomato plants at night when a frost is expected, or on clear, still nights, using plastic sheets, baskets, or other materials.

GROWING WINTER TOMATOES IN A SUNNY WINDOW

While you won't harvest bushel-baskets of tomatoes from plants grown in a sunny window, the fruits that do grow may be all the more delicious because of their scarcity. And it's safe to say that you'll be one of the few in your circle to have "edible houseplants," if you follow the suggestions below.

Get the Right Variety

Don't choose a vigorous variety for indoor growing. Much more success can be achieved with small plants. Varieties bred for greenhouse growing are also fine for a sunny window. Good vari-

eties include 'Pixie Hybrid,' 'Patio,' 'Tiny Tim,' and 'Small Fry.'

'Pixie Hybrid'

Start in September

Start plants from seed indoors early in September, using the methods outlined in Chapter 4, or take root cuttings from plants in the garden (just snap off 6-inch-long shoot-tips, put them in a glass of water, and pot them when they root.) All moveable patio plants can also be taken inside.

Most of the containers mentioned in Chapter 4 can be used for potting indoor tomato plants. The main difference is that they must be set in a tray, pan, or dish to catch drainage water. Rest the tray on a mat or a magazine so that it won't mar the finish it rests on. The pot in the tray should be raised slightly from the bottom by resting it on small stones, marble chips, or strips of wood so that the pot doesn't sit in water.

Use the Right Container Mix

Of the container mixes mentioned in Chapter 4, the USDA vermiculite mix is best for indoor tomatoes. But prepared potting soil is good, too. Just be sure not to bring garden soil indoors as it dries out too quickly and often contains pests and diseases.

Good Light

Light is the most important factor in indoor tomato growing. A sunny window facing south is almost essential for any real success. An easterly window is the second choice and a westerly or northerly window is virtually useless. On dark days you can give your plants an extra dose of light by putting them about a foot away from an ordinary lamp. Incandescent lights don't have sunlight's range of light waves, but will help some.

Right Temperature

Maintain a temperature of from 65°F to 75°F during the day and from 60°F to 65°F at night.

Space plants about one foot from the window, and pull the shade or drapes at night to give them more warmth. Do not put the plants close to a radiator or heater. Too much direct heat will harm them more than cold.

Air Circulation

Be sure that there is good air circulation in the room, even if you only open a window or door a few minutes every day for ventilation.

Water and Fertilize

Water and fertilize plants as described for outdoor container plants (see Chapter 4). If you are away for any length of time, have someone water the plants or buy an automatic watering system.

Prune...Maybe

If small varieties are used, there will be little need to prune. If plants do grow too tall, you'll have to prune every week, pinching back new growth so that the tops don't grow out of balance with the relatively small root systems in the containers.

Pollination

Tomatoes are self-pollinated and indoors they have to be tapped firmly or even vibrated with a electric toothbrush when new blossoms appear so that the pollen will scatter. You can also spray the blossoms with a fruit-setting hormone.

Turn the Plants

As a final tip, remember to rotate tomato plants growing in windows about 90°F in the same direction once a week, if possible. The plants will grow more symmetrically this way.

GROWING WINTER TOMATOES INDOORS UNDER ARTIFICIAL LIGHTS

Raising winter tomatoes indoors under fluorescent lights such as Gro-Light™ or Gro-Lux™ is the only solution for those without a sunny enough window. No matter how much sun a window gets, plants grown under artificial lights will produce far more fruit than those growing in any window. The lights can be set up anywhere in the house where temperatures are suitable—in a large, empty closet, or in the basement, attic, or on shelves in the living room.

Treat plants grown under fluorescent lights the same as plants growing in a window. Keep the plants about 6 inches from the lights. Be generous with the light, too, giving plants 16 to 18 hours of it daily. Automatic timers are available that will enable you to do this more consistently when at home or away. It's also a good idea to buy a wide reflector that attaches to the grow-lights as it focuses more light onto the plants. White- or aluminum-painted backgrounds will reflect light, too, as will small mirrors placed under the plants.

GROWING TOMATOES IN THE GREENHOUSE

Anyone fortunate enough to have a heated greenhouse can grow tomatoes there all year round. You'll be most successful if you use tomato varieties bred specifically for greenhouse culture, especially the small-fruited types, such as the following:

All small-fruited 'cherry' types
'Bay State'
'Burpee Early Hybrid'
'Caro Rich'
'Doublerich'
'Fireball'
'Floraloud'
'Homestead'
'Manapal'
'Manalucie'
'Marglobe'
'New Yorker'
'Rutgers'
'San Marzano'
'Toy Boy'
'Vendor'

Caring for tomato plants in the greenhouse is more difficult than caring for plants grown outdoors. You must provide good ventilation and clean conditions as diseases can quickly become enormous problems in a greenhouse that does not provide these conditions. The following pointers will help you grow better tomatoes under glass.

Use a Soilless Mix

Use a fresh, soil-free planting medium to avoid bringing soil-borne diseases into the greenhouse. Some tomato growers plant tomatoes right in the potting soil bags. Just lay the bags flat, cut holes in the top, and plant.

Use the Right Varieties

Select greenhouse varieties or disease-resistant types for greenhouse growing.

Rotate Crops

If you plant directly in the ground, rotate greenhouse tomatoes every year, never planting them in soil where tomatoes, potatoes, peppers, or eggplants once grew. Some growers use a greenhouse they can move to a fresh patch of soil every year.

Produce Two Crops

Most growers of greenhouse tomatoes produce a spring and fall crop. The spring crop is easier to grow and yields are considerably higher. This is due to the improved light and other conditions in the spring and early summer compared to the fall and early winter. The spring crop is seeded in late December or early January and the fall crop is started in late June and early July.

Temperature

The best temperatures for growing tomatoes in the greenhouse range from 70°F to 75°F in the daytime and 60°F to 70°F at night. Don't let daytime temperatures exceed 85°F or nighttime temperatures drop below 60°F.

Ventilation

Make certain that the greenhouse is properly ventilated. Open the vents on hot days, and follow all other pertinent directions for greenhouse operation as noted in your owner's manual.

Fertilize

Fertilize tomato plants once every 2 or 3 weeks with a balanced liquid fertilizer.

Mulch

Use black plastic mulch to keep things clean and prevent soil-borne diseases from splashing up on the plants.

Water

Water plants whenever the soil is dry to the depth of about one inch. Don't splash plants with dirt and never water the foliage on greenhouse plants, especially late in the day when they won't have a chance to dry off by night.

Prune

To conserve room, prune plants to a single or double stem as described in Chapter 2. Stake vigorous varieties just as you would outside. Another technique is to stretch wire between two stakes 7 to 8 feet high over a row of plants. Then drop string from the wire to each plant so that it is loose enough to allow for plant growth.

As the plant grows, carefully train it upward by twisting it around the string.

Encourage Pollination

Greenhouse tomatoes can't be pollinated by insects or wind, so they must be pollinated by artificial means. Shake those plants with blossoms on them or vibrate them with an electric toothbrush every morning.

Practice Sanitary Habits

Practice the same good sanitary habits in the greenhouse that you would in the garden. For example, never smoke cigarettes or bring tobacco into the greenhouse when tending plants. This could cause the dreaded tobacco mosaic virus to spread.

Chapter 6

Controlling Common Problems

Taking good care of your tomato plants so they grow healthy foliage, stems, roots, and, of course, fruits is the best way to help your plants resist most pest and disease problems. Toward this end, you'll want to give your

tomato plants good, loamy soil that drains well, plenty of sunlight, good mulching, proper watering, and proper spacing so that each plant has adequate air circulation. Another way to reduce disease and pest damage is to rotate the crops where you plant your tomato plants.

You can also avoid many problems by planting tomato varieties that are resistant to diseases and nematodes. If you've had problems growing tomatoes before because of certain diseases, select a variety resistant to those diseases. No tomato variety is resistant to all diseases, but hundreds of varieties have some resistance against one or more diseases.

BENEFICIAL INSECTS

Scientists estimate that 99 percent of the 1.6 million known insect species are beneficial for or harmless to plants. The same applies to birds and other wildlife. Don't harm insects and other creatures that aren't harming your plants. Learn which are helpful to tomato plants. You can encourage them to come to your garden by providing plants they like or by hanging commercial lures. You can purchase beneficial insects such as ladybugs, praying mantises, and trichogramma wasps to release into your garden through many of the organic gardening catalogs, or check garden magazines for ads. One pint of ladybugs contains about 10,000 of the little garden helpers.

The Good Guys in the Garden

Here is a list of some of the "good guys" you may encounter in your garden. For a more extensive selection, you may want to research organic gardeners' supply companies. Many of the insects listed below can be purchased in their dormant stages through organic garden supply companies.

• **Assassin Bugs.** These long-legged, brown insects are ³/₄ inch long, with wings that fold above the body. They do bite people if provoked, but will happily devour a good many harmful insects, grabbing them by the front legs and "assassinating" them.

• **Assassin Flies.** These hairy black-and-gray flies are about 1 inch long with yellowish legs. They prey on many insects.

• **Birds.** Birds rarely bother tomatoes, and their good qualities far outnumber any bad habits. Little birds, especially, are apt to be meat-eaters and feed voraciously on slugs, aphids, and other harmful bugs.

• **Centipedes.** These fat, brown, many-legged creatures have one pair of legs per segment (unlike the slightly harmful millipede, which has 2 pairs per segment). Centipedes often live under rocks. They dine on several pests, including slugs and snails.

• **Damsel Bugs.** These resemble the assassin bugs but are only about half their size. They feed on aphids and other small, soft-bodied insects.

• **Doodlebugs.** These plump, brown insects are known for their forceplike jaws. Doodlebugs destroy ants, which often encourage aphids. They dig a cone-shaped hole in the ground, hide at the bottom, and wait until an ant falls into their trap.

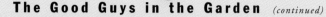

The Good Guys in the Garden *(continued)*

• **Dragonflies.** These insects are 2 inches or longer with big eyes and transparent wings. They catch their prey—other insects—in the air.

• **Flower Flies.** These small, ³/₈-inch-long insects resemble bees. Flower flies hover over flowers and catch aphids and other harmful insects.

• **Lacewings.** These delicate, ³/₄-inch-long, pale-green insects with golden eyes have filmy wings twice the size of their bodies. Lacewing larvae are also valuable in the garden because they eat troublesome insects. They are about ¹/₃ inch long, yellowish, and torpedo-shaped, with hairs on the body, and jaws shaped like forceps. These larvae are called "aphid lions" because of the prodigious numbers of aphids they eat. Lacewing larvae are also valuable because they devour hard-to-kill mites and other insects.

• **Ladybugs.** Ladybugs are perhaps the best-known beneficial insect with some 350 species worldwide. They are small, yellow-to-orange beetles with black spots on their backs. They feed on aphids, mites, whiteflies, scale insects, and the eggs of other insects.

• **Praying Mantis.** The praying mantis is also a familiar insect and huge by insect standards, ranging from 4 to 6 inches long. They are greenish or brown and have triangular heads that they turn from side to side. Their front legs are held in a "praying" position, ready to seize other insects, their only food source.

• **Spiders.** However you may feel about spiders, they destroy numerous garden pests. Most spiders are harmless to people.

• **Toads.** Toads are great garden helpers. Keep a pet toad in your garden to devour all kinds of pests, including cutworms, slugs, and stink bugs. Attract toads with a small dish filled with water in a shady part of the garden, and a little home for the toad in the form of an upside-down flower pot with one side propped up so the toad can enter and leave.

• **Trichogramma Wasps.** These are tiny wasps that deposit their eggs in the eggs of more than 200 harmful insects. When they hatch, they feed on the pest's eggs, preventing them from hatching. These wasps do not bite humans, and do not resemble their larger cousins.

COMPANION PLANTS

Companion plants can keep troublesome insects from harming your tomatoes. For example, planting marigolds will help deter meadow nematodes, as mentioned earlier in the book, and the garlic plant also works as a repellent against many insects. Certain plants either repel insects from the general area, attract helper insects to eat the pests, or attract the pest insects so that you can trap or destroy them. The plants listed below are by no means all the useful companion plants there are. Experiment with other plants and watch for combinations that seem to work in your garden. Beneficial plants are also discussed under the specific pests that they help fight in the "Most Unwanted" list, this chapter.

Trapping by Example

Trap plants act as a lure, attracting bugs to another plant instead of the one you are protecting. For example, several trap plants successful in attracting Japanese beetles away from tomatoes are larkspur and white geraniums. When the beetles congregate on these plants, you can shake them into a bag and destroy them.

Repellent Plants

Companion plants that repel insects from the tomato patch include marigolds, which cut down on harmful nematodes in the soil and begonias, which get rid of aphids. Other plants that repel aphids are nasturtiums, garlic, chives, and rhubarb.

Attracting Plants

Certain plants provide food or homes for small garden helpers. Flowers, for example, provide nectar for tiny, non-biting wasps that lay their eggs on pests' eggs. Buckwheat, mints, and daisies are all good choices, too.

FIRST THINGS FIRST

Once you are assured that the plant's basic needs are provided for, make your eyes your first line of defense against pests and diseases. Check your

Don't be afraid to mix flowers in with your tomatoes. Marigolds are an especially good companion for tomatoes, because they help control root-knot nematodes.

plants often, looking carefully at the foliage (including the undersides of leaves, stems, and flowers) for signs of any potential disease or pest. Look for the symptoms of insect and disease presence, noting any spots, wilting, or yellow leaves, as well as the signs of insect tracks or "honeydew," a sticky substance secreted by aphids and other insects. You'll usually find the damage and not the culprit since most insects work under cover of night. You may catch the insect in the act if you're willing to return to the tomato patch after dark with a flashlight. Examine any insect or symptom you find (place insects in a clear plastic bag) with a magnifying glass, if you have one.

Use the "Most Unwanted" list and the "Good Guys in the Garden" list to help identify bugs and diseases you don't recognize. If you still can't identify a bug or a symptom (spots, yellowing leaves, for example) and the general suggestions below don't seem to help, you may want to take your specimen (leaf or bug in a bag) to your local garden center or extension agent for identification.

There are many very effective ways to eliminate pest and disease problems without resorting to spraying or dusting with harmful chemicals. You'll find specific suggestions listed after the insect and disease names in the "Most Unwanted" list in this chapter. Even if you're not quite sure exactly of the specific problem facing your plant, the steps outlined below will help you eliminate many of the pests and problems in the garden:

- Large, plant-chewing insects can be hand-picked—use rubber gloves if you're queasy about touching them—and then dropped into a tin of soapy water. Let them drown, then dump it in the compost.

- A strong spray of water can knock off smaller insects, such as aphids, drowning them or making them think twice about their choice of home.

- Pull up a very sick or insect-infested plant and seal it in a plastic garbage bag to put out with the trash. This nips a problem in the bud, and prevents it from spreading. Chances are the plant would never really produce well, even if you got it cleaned up. Putting such

plants in the compost isn't a good idea unless you can bury them in the center of a hot-to-the-touch, actively composting pile. You may want to take a close look at the roots before you give it the heave-ho for signs of insect damage or disease.

CONVENTIONAL PEST CONTROLS

While there are many effective, broad-spectrum, synthetic pesticides on the market today, please don't spray or dust just for good measure. Wait until you have a problem, then target that problem. If you do choose to apply a pesticide, be sure to read and follow all the cautions listed on the label concerning mixing, applying, storing, and disposing of the product.

ORGANIC PEST CONTROLS

Many gardeners are concerned about putting long-lasting poisons on their food and choose not to use them at all. They prefer to use control measures that are not poisonous (some of which are mentioned above) or natural poisons that break down rapidly into harmless substances after they are applied to plants. These are often referred to as "organic" controls and can be purchased at your local garden center or ordered from a nursery mail order company. Others you can even make yourself. While all of the controls listed here are safe and effective when used as directed, it is important to remember that "organic" doesn't mean harmless. Read and follow the cautions you find on any product's label.

Selection of Organic Pest Controls

Here is a listing of some of the more common organic controls available.

- **Bacillus thuringiensis (Bt).** Available under the brand names Dipel, Biotrol, BT, and Thuricide, this product is very effective against cutworms and tomato hornworms. These bacteria make such pests sick, but do not affect other pests or larger animals. Use granules or a soil drench for soil-dwelling pests, sprays to control leaf-chewing pests. Mix and apply according to the label, adding a few drops of soap and molasses to the solution. Apply every few days for best results.

- **Baking soda.** Sodium bicarbonate, or baking soda, is a preventative fungicide that remains active until rain washes it from the leaves. Mix 1 teaspoon of baking soda and ¼ teaspoon of liquid soap in 1 quart of water, and spray plants weekly or after each rain to prevent fungal diseases from spreading.

- **Bordeaux mix.** This fungicide is a combination of copper sulfate and lime. Spray plants according to the instructions on the package label.

- **Copper.** Copper is a natural mineral and is also a potent fungicide. Purchase a commercial copper spray, and use it according to the instructions on the package label. Avoid spraying the soil as much as possible, since copper is harmful to garden helpers living in the soil, including earthworms. See also Bordeaux mix.

- **Diatomaceous earth.** This natural product is made from the fossilized shells of tiny sea creatures. It has many sharp points too small for the human finger to feel, but large enough to poke holes in pests, such as slugs and aphids. Buy natural, not pool-grade, diatomaceous earth. Dust on plants or surrounding soil.

- **Milky disease spores.** Sold as "Doom" or "milky spore," this bacterial insecticide destroys Japanese beetle grubs and other insects that live in the soil for part of their lives. It works best when it is applied over acres of lawn. It has no effect on the adult beetles themselves.

- **Neem.** A natural insecticide and fungicide made from the seeds of a tropical tree, Neem kills a wide range of pest insects. Of all the natural plant-derived pesticides, neem is probably the safest choice because it won't harm beneficial insects and larger animals.

- **Oil.** Petroleum and vegetable oils kill insects by smothering them. Purchase a commercial oil spray and prepare it according to the label or make your own mix of 1 tablespoon vegetable oil and ¼ teaspoon liquid soap with 1 quart water. Shake vigorously and spray plants.

- **Pyrethrum.** This natural pesticide is made from the ground flowers of pyrethrum daisies. It kills many chewing and sucking insects. Resort to it only after water and/or soapy water sprays have not worked. Apply according to the manufacturer's instructions.

- **Rotenone.** Rotenone is another natural pesticide, this one derived from a tropical plant. It is of low toxicity to humans and kills many types of chewing insects such as beetles. Rotenone works slowly, lasting about 1 week. Rotenone and pyrethrum are often sold mixed together. Apply according to the manufacturer's instructions.

- **Soap.** Soapy water sprayed or painted on tomato plants serves as a good general-purpose insect repellent. Green soap or soaps made with fish or coconut oils are best; any will do, but avoid detergents. Commercial insecticidal soaps are available. Follow instructions on the package label or use 1 to 3 teaspoons of household soap per gallon of water. Test soap spray on a few leaves first, and wait a day. If leaves aren't scorched, spray the whole plant. If they are, dilute the spray with water, and test again.

- **Water.** A strong, fine hose spray of water will kill aphids and many other insects, or knock them off the plants.

Two Organic Controls That Do More Harm Than Good

Tobacco dust is sometimes sold as an organic control, but it is quite poisonous and doesn't break down quickly. For that reason alone, many organic gardeners don't use it. Don't use it on tomatoes because it might carry and infect your plants with tobacco mosaic virus. Another harmful control are mothballs, which are also quite poisonous and long-lasting.

"MOST UNWANTED" TOMATO PROBLEMS

Don't let the size of this list scare you. Many gardeners have raised tomatoes for years and never encountered more than a few of the many potential problems that exist. If you choose suitable varieties for your climate and purposes, and provide good growing conditions, care, and maintenance, you can greatly reduce your exposure to problems.

It's perfectly natural to see some damage on the plants, and don't panic if you notice a chewed leaf or other damage on one of your plants. Most likely the plant will survive and produce admirably, especially if steps are taken to help it

Homemade Pest Sprays

There are many home-grown remedies for repelling pests in the garden that are natural, nontoxic, and won't harm your plants or the soil. The following are a few combinations you might want to try. Add a few drops of liquid soap to the mixes so that they will cling to the plants. Many strong-scented leaves are also effective as repellents, such as geranium leaves and mint. Add them to to any of these mixes. Experiment and see what works for you.

- **Compost Tea.** A spadeful of compost soaked in 1 bucket of water for an hour or so, strained, and sprinkled over plants will fertilize them, repels a number of insects, and may even make the plants more disease- and frost-resistant.

- **Garlic-Pepper-Soap Spray.** Blend together 4 crushed cloves of garlic, 4 tablespoons of hot red pepper (cayenne), one cake of strong soap, and 1 cup of hot water. Dissolve in 2 gallons of hot water (the size of most watering cans), cool, and use for a general insect spray.

- **Garlic Spray.** Press 1 garlic clove and mix the oily juice with 1 gallon water for an all-purpose spray.

- **Ground Hot Pepper.** Dust on tomato plants for protection against several insects and larger animal pests.

- **Hot Pepper Spray.** Grind hot pepper pods and mix with an equal amount of water and a little soap for use against tomato worms.

- **Onion Spray.** Grind fresh onions very finely in a blender or by hand, and mix 1 tablespoon onions with 1 pint water for an all-purpose spray.

- **Pickled Peppers.** One pint (or peck) of pickled peppers put through a blender and sprinkled over plants makes a good general insecticide.

- **Rhubarb Leaves.** Soak 3 pounds of torn-up leaves in 3 quarts of water for 1 hour, strain, and sprinkle over plants infected with aphids.

---

along. Other problems are, unfortunately, not so easily fixed. Experience is a great teacher, and the next time you encounter the same problem, you'll probably be better equipped to handle it and perhaps know how to avoid it.

Anthracnose

This is a rot disease that attacks ripe tomatoes when plants are grown in infertile, poorly drained soil. Anthracnose lesions appear on the fruits and are small, circular, slightly sunken, water-soaked spots that grow darker and deeper, often developing ring markings.

Controls: Dispose of all diseased fruits so that they don't spread the disease. Cover any bare soil with mulch to prevent soil splashing up on the plant. Organic control is copper or Bordeaux mixture. Chemical control is a dusting with Zineb™. Enrich the soil and improve drainage;

rotate crops from year to year; clean up debris in the garden; and protect against rain splash by mulching properly.

Aphids

Aphids are smaller than ⅛-inch round, and are soft-bodied plant lice ranging from pale pink to deep green in color. They tend to cluster on tender stems and undersides of tomato leaves, sucking out plant juices and causing leaves to curl. Ants often spread aphids (which they keep as "milk cows" for the sweet secretion they exude) from plant to plant.

Controls: Organic controls are a strong spray of water, or a soap spray, if water doesn't work. A chemical control of aphids is never necessary. Try mulching with aluminum foil, which confuses flying aphids. Keep the soil well-fertilized and evenly moist. Plant aphid-repellent plants, such as nasturtiums, garlic, chives, and rhubarb.

Bacterial Canker

The first symptoms of this disease caused by contaminated seed-bed soil and infected seeds are wilting, browning, and rolling of leaves on the side of the plant. The fruit becomes infected and shows "birds-eye" spots, which are whitish-brown spots with a white halo around them.

Controls: Destroy infected fruit. Buy plants or seeds from a reputable source; rotate crops, because the disease can live in the soil a full year; keep the garden clean; and especially don't dig tomatoes or potatoes, or their foliage, into the garden—these can harbor the bacterial canker.

Bacterial Spot

Bacterial spot is common during warm, rainy seasons. Lesions are small, dark, slightly raised dots (often with a water-soaked border) that can reach ¼ inch in size. Wind-blown rain spreads the disease.

Controls: Destroy infected fruit. Cover any bare soil with mulch. Buy plants or seeds from a reputable source next year; rotate crops, because the disease can live in the soil a full year; keep the garden clean; and especially don't dig tomatoes or potatoes, or their foliage, into the garden—these can harbor the bacterial canker.

Bacterial Wilt

Often called "brown rot," this disease spreads quickly, killing the entire plant without visible damage, such as spotting or yellowing of leaves. Stems infected with bacterial wilt will reveal water-soaked pith at the ground level and emit a slimy substance when pressed. This substance distinguishes bacterial wilt from fusarium and verticillium wilts.

Controls: Pull and bag affected plants and discard with the trash. Don't grow tomatoes or any related crops for 4 to 5 years in the area where this disease occurs; grow seedlings in pasteurized soil; and use disease-resistant varieties.

Birds

Birds rarely bother tomatoes.

Controls: If they are a problem, cover the plants with bird netting.

Blister Beetles

About 1 inch long, these gray, red, black, or striped beetles feed on tomato leaves.

Controls: The best way to combat these busy beetles is to hand pick them off plants and crush them. Be sure to wear gloves because, as their name implies, they can blister skin with a secretion called "cantharadine."

Blossom Drop

A temperature problem, rather than a disease, blossom drop most often occurs in hot, dry periods, and during unexpected periods of cold, rainy weather. Large-fruited varieties are especially susceptible to this problem. Other diseases listed here cause blossom drop too, but in those cases the diseases are always accompanied by other symptoms.

Controls: The problem will usually resolve itself when the weather returns to normal. Keep plants mulched, and the soil evenly moist, and do not feed plants large amounts of nitrogen, which encourages green growth at the expense of fruiting. Grow resistant varieties in hot, dry climates such as the Southwest; shake the plants daily to encourage fruit set.

Blossom-end Rot

A condition caused by moisture fluctuations and a lack of calcium uptake from the soil during dry conditions, blossom-end rot first shows up as a slight water-soaked area near the blossom end of the fruit. This sunken, leathery lesion turns black and enlarges, growing eventually to encompass half of the tomato. It often appears on the first fruits of tomato plants set early in cold soils, or after a long, dry spell.

Controls: Keep soil moisture consistent by mulching and careful irrigation; make sure the ground is well-drained to allow for proper root development; avoid cultivating closer than one foot from plants to avoid root pruning; avoid giving plants heavy dosages of nitrogen, which aggravates calcium deficiency in the soil; have soil tested for calcium deficiency, excess salts, and excess alkalinity, which are all causative factors; and ask your state agricultural extension service for corrective recommendations. Staked plants are less affected by blossom-end rot than unstaked ones. There are several resistant varieties.

Buckeye Rot

This fungal disease affects only tomato fruits, causing water-soaked brown or grayish-green spots near the blossom end of the fruit, especially where it touches the soil.

Controls: Mulch under plants to cover any bare soil. Make sure the ground is well drained; take care in watering or mulching plants so that they won't be splashed by soil; stake plants so that fruits will not touch the soil; and rotate crops from year to year.

Catfacing

This condition shows up as badly malformed and scarred fruit—some people think these look like a cat's face—at the blossom end of the tomatoes. Catfacing appears as bands of scar tissue, swollen bulges, and puckering of fruits. Extremes of heat and cold, drought, or pesticide injury can all cause abnormal development of the tomato flower, resulting in catfacing. Remember that some old varieties are oddly shaped naturally.

Controls: Keep soil evenly moist; the condition should not appear on future fruit. Hybrid varieties are not as susceptible as older varieties.

Chlorosis

Chlorosis appears as yellow or pale leaves all over a tomato plant, especially when the yellow is between greener leaf veins. This results from excess lime (alkaline soil) or insufficient iron in the soil.

Controls: Spraying plants with compost tea, dilute liquid fertilizer, or a chelated iron product may help green them up. Have a soil-acidity test made and, if the soil is alkaline, add iron sulfate.

Cloudy Spot

A blemish on both green and ripe fruits caused by the feeding punctures of stink bugs, on green fruits, characterized by cream-colored, $1/8$- to $1/4$-inch-round spots that become yellowish spots on ripening fruits.

Controls: *See Stink bugs.*

Collar Rot

Young transplants are affected with this rot disease at the surface of the soil.

Controls: Fertile soil, well enriched with compost, and kept moist, but not soggy. Dip transplants in compost tea or a Meneb™ solution before planting.

Corn borers

Corn borers are slender, 1-inch-long or longer, pinkish grubs that are the larvae of a brown moth. They only occasionally eat tomato leaves and fruit.

Controls: Crush the caterpillars and the masses of corn borer eggs laid on the undersides of leaves. Rotenone spray is also somewhat effective. Don't plant tomatoes near corn, if possible.

Cracking

Cracks in fruit occur after heavy rains or heavy irrigation, especially when the soil has not been kept evenly moist. The growth cracks can be circular or radial. Once cracks occur, they often become infected with various rots.

Controls: Remove tomatoes from the vine and use them when they first crack; keep soil evenly moist; and plant crack-resistant varieties.

Cucumber Mosaic

A virus disease that causes misshapen, shoestring-type leaves and severe stunting in young plants, this is spread by aphids that carry it from nearby weeds, flowers, and vegetables.

Controls: Pull up and destroy infected plants. Keep the garden free of weeds; control aphids.

Curly Top

A virus disease that causes leaves to curl and twist upward on mature plants, this is spread by leaf-hoppers moving from plant to plant.

Controls: Pull up and destroy infected plants. Keep the garden free of weeds; control aphids. Shade healthy plants with muslin tents to make them less attractive to leaf-hoppers. Late tomato varieties aren't as susceptible as early ones.

Cutworms

Smooth gray, black, brownish, or greenish caterpillars usually found curled up just under the top layer of soil, cutworms cut off young plants evenly at the surface of the ground (as opposed to uneven cuts, which indicate rabbit damage) and are generally an early-season problem.

Controls: You can protect intact plants by placing stiff, 3-inch-tall cardboard collars around plants at ground level (1 inch into the soil and 2 inches above it) so that cutworms can't reach the plant stems. Keeping the garden clean will give adult cutworms fewer places to lay eggs.

Bacillus thuringiensis (Bt) is available in most garden centers and controls cutworms when sprinkled on the soil.

Damping-off

This fungal disease causes seedlings to flop over in their flats with their stems rotted through at the soil line.

Controls: Plant seeds in soilless planting medium. Keep soil moist, but never soggy. Sow seeds thinly, and thin as recommended.

Deer

Deer have no special affinity for tomatoes, but hungry deer may eat anything and they may step on the plants.

Controls: If deer are a problem in your garden, wire fencing at least 7 feet tall is often the only sure protection, though a dog that marks the boundaries will also provide some control. Some gardeners have tried lining the garden with clothes drenched with perspiration to warn of man's presence. There are also several commercial taste and scent repellents for use against deer, including one that emits the scent of a mountain lion. Egg yolks or cayenne pepper mixed with water and sprayed on plants may also discourage nibbling deer.

Dogs and Cats

Most dogs and cats have little interest in tomatoes.

Controls: Cover young plants with wire cages to keep them from being sat on or dug up. There are also a number of natural repellent products on the market that are designed to repel dogs and cats.

Early Blight

Primarily a foliage blight caused by a fungus, early blight also causes fruit rot around tomato fruit stems in late fall. Early blight is characterized by brown irregular spots with concentric rings in a target pattern on the older, lower leaves. These spots soon enlarge to up to 1/2 inch in diameter, run together, and cause the leaves to turn brown and usually drop off. Often all the leaves drop off the lower half of the plant. Spotting and girdling of the stems also takes place. Fruits exposed to more sun as the leaves drop off are susceptible to sun-scald. When the fruits are attacked by early blight, they are useless.

Controls: Organic controls are copper or Bordeaux mixture. Chemical control is Maneb fungicide. Clean up all plants that were affected at the end of the season, as early blight fungus over-winters in old tomato debris and weeds; buy commercial seed, which is unlikely to be infected with the fungus; and use a variety such as Manalucie, which is somewhat resistant.

Earwigs

These 1-inch-long or longer, brown or black insects with or without wings have a pincer-like tail. Earwigs sometimes damage leaves on young tomato plants.

Controls: They like to gather under cover and can be trapped and destroyed by laying boards on the soil and lifting them daily to pick up the critters. Encourage wild birds to nest near your garden, because they enjoy earwigs for breakfast. Sea sand spread around plants repels earwigs, as does diatomaceous earth, or tea leaves mixed equally with soil and peat moss. Commercial earwig bait used according to the manufacturer's directions also kills the pests.

Flea Beetles

Smaller than 1/8 inch long, these brown to black jumping beetles make small, round holes in young tomato leaves. They usually leave tomatoes early in the season, before they have done any irreparable harm. Their larvae are small white worms which feed on the roots of plants.

Controls: If flea beetles are a real problem, you can spray plants with soapy water. Keep the garden weed-free, so that they can't nest in them and reproduce. Try planting basil, which repels the beetles, near the tomatoes.

Fruit Rot

There are many minor tomato fruit rots—most of them are only a problem if fruits have punctures in them.

Controls: Prevent insect damage. Check harvested tomatoes for small holes. If they have any, use the tomatoes at once.

Fusarium Wilt

A common disease caused by a fungus that can live in the soil many years, this infection occurs only when soil temperature reaches 75°F to 85°F. Symptoms are yellowing of the older, lower leaves, which soon die. Then other leaves up to the top leaves yellow and wilt. Eventually, the entire plant wilts. Infection occurs through the root hairs, enters the vascular system, and blocks the flow of water and nutrients into the plant. A brown, discolored streak forms about 1/8 inch under the surface of the main stem and usually extends to the top of the plant. You can locate this symptom by slicing the stem near the soil line.

Controls: Pull up and destroy wilting plants when the soil is moist. If you have had fusarium wilt in the garden, don't plant tomatoes, peppers, eggplants, or potatoes in the same place more than once in 4 years. Buy seedlings grown in clean soil, use sterilized soil to grow your own seedlings, and keep the garden clean of weeds and refuse. By far the best precaution against fusarium wilt is to buy one of the many resistant varieties available.

Ghost Spot

Characterized by small white circles surrounding a green center on the fruit surface, this fungal disease usually appears on the shoulders of small green tomatoes. Fruits generally develop to normal size and shape, and are good to eat, but blemished.

Controls: If the disease is prevalent in your area, put out tomatoes after cool, damp conditions have passed for the season; don't plant tomatoes in any area of the garden where ghost spot has occurred.

Gophers

Gophers are voracious plant eaters and have the dubious distinction of tunneling up to a plant, eating the roots, then pulling the plant down into the hole to devour it. Occasionally, you will see a plant shaking wildly, and getting shorter as you watch.

Controls: Trenching deeply around the garden and installing a wire mesh barrier below the soil line may keep them out of the garden. Containers are another way to thwart them. *See also controls for Moles.*

Gray Leaf Spot

Small grayish-brown spots on the undersides of leaves characterize this fungal disease which occurs mainly in the Southeast. As the disease progresses, the leaves yellow and drop, resulting in low fruit yield.

Controls: If you have had gray leaf spot on tomatoes, be sure to remove and destroy all plants in the garden at the end of the season, for the fungus is carried over on the remains of discarded plants. Plant resistant varieties.

Graywall

This viral disease results in blotchy ripening of fruit with internal browning.

Controls: Shaded fruit are more affected, so removing some leaves and thinning plants may reduce the problem. Avoid high-nitrogen fertilizers that encourage leafy growth. Keep the garden weed-free to eliminate sources of the virus. Plant resistant varieties

Hard Core

This condition shows up as tomatoes with hard centers that are unpalatable.

Controls: Hard core is caused by temperature fluctuations, especially low night temperatures. It should pass as the season warms.

Japanese Beetles

The adults are shiny green and bronze, $1/2$-inch-long, brown-winged insects. Japanese beetles, common east and west of the Rockies, feed on tomato foliage.

Controls: Try hand-picking them (hold a tray under the plant, as they tend to drop off when disturbed) and drowning them in soapy water. There are commercial traps available, but if you choose to use them be sure to put them as far away from your garden as possible as they often seem to attract more beetles than they nab. To control severe infestations, spray with Rotenone or a pesticide labeled for them. Treat large areas of lawn with milky disease spores to reduce the population next year.

Late Blight

A fungal disease that often occurs during long periods of muggy weather with cool nights, this blight shows up as greasy black areas that appear on the leaf-margins, soon consuming the entire leaf. A fine gray mold can be seen on the underside of the leaf during wet periods. Both green and ripe fruits become corky brown on their surfaces and take on a texture resembling an orange peel. The rot remains firm but makes the fruit inedible.

Controls: Remove plants at the first sign of disease, seal them in plastic bags, and discard them with the trash to keep the disease from spreading. You can also try spraying mildly infected plants with Bordeaux mixture or Zineb. Don't plant tomatoes near potatoes, which can become blighted and spread the disease; don't compost either infected potato or tomato plants. Plant resistant varieties.

Leaf Mold

A fungal disease with symptoms of yellowish or greenish spots, followed by purple mold growth on leaves, this usually occurs at its worst in damp, rainy weather.

Controls: Keep plant leaves dry and water only the soil. Stake plants and thin them out to increase air circulation. Plant resistant varieties.

Leaf Roll and Curl

A condition that commonly occurs in wet spring weather, especially on plants set in poorly drained soil. Some early tomato varieties have curlier leaves by nature. Close cultivation or pruning may also cause the condition.

Controls: Leaf roll is really nothing much to worry about, because as temperatures rise and soils dry out, the symptoms disappear and normal growth resumes. No damage is done to fruits that develop later. Plant on well-drained soil, mulch with straw, and cultivate shallowly to avoid damaging plant roots.

Leafhoppers

Up to $1/5$-inch-long, slender, pale green to brown, wedge-shaped, soft-bodied insects, these suck juice from the undersides of tomato leaves and stems. You'll notice leafhoppers by the dozens if they're present. Curled tomato leaves with dark tips are evidence of their ravaging. Leafhoppers are most bothersome west of the Rockies, where they are called Beet Leafhoppers.

Controls: Cover young plants with floating row cover to keep the pests off early in the season. Spray plants with soapy water. Don't plant tomatoes near beets.

Mice

Mice can sometimes be a problem if you use a straw-like mulch.

Controls: Pull mulch a few inches away from stems. Garlic planted nearby can help repel them. Traps and poisons can be set out for them if they are a big problem. *See also controls for Moles.*

Mites

A certain type of tiny mites will cause tomato leaves to develop a white, fuzzy look. They are usually a problem in the Southeast and on the Pacific Coast.

Controls: Mites thrive in dry, hot, dusty conditions. Spraying plants with plain water often gets rid of them; soapy water is a bit stronger.

Moles

Moles are meat-eaters and have no interest in tomatoes. In fact, they eat up soil-dwelling pests that might bother tomatoes. But the tunnels moles make can be bothersome underfoot, and worse, can serve as runways for mice and voles that will eat plants.

Controls: Garlic planted in the garden repels moles, and castor oil sprinkled around plants helps, too. There are commercial products you can water into the soil that repel moles. Fencing below the soil line can keep them out altogether.

Nematodes

These are tiny, microscopic worms. From the gardener's point of view, there are good nematodes and bad nematodes. Good nematodes feed on soil-dwelling pests. These can be purchased and applied to garden soil. On the other hand, bad nematodes such as root-knot nematodes feed on plant roots and stunt plants. They are especially troublesome to tomatoes in the South, causing stunted plants and leaving swellings (galls) on plant roots that contain their eggs.

Controls: Nematodes are usually controlled by rotating crops and never growing tomatoes or related crops such as potatoes and eggplant in the same space for more than two years so that nematodes can't build up in the soil, or by planting one of the many nematode-resistant tomato varieties. Another control is to keep the soil well supplied with humus by digging in organic matter. Marigolds (especially African marigolds) planted near tomatoes will exude a substance from their roots that will repel nematodes up to a year after planting.

Pinworms

Up to $1/4$ inch long, these gray to green, brown-headed, slender worms tunnel into tomato stems and fruit and web leaves together. Pinworms are most common in the South and California.

Controls: Hand pick and drop worms into soapy water to drown them. Also try garlic spray to repel them.

Potato Beetles

The adults are yellow and black, striped, hard-shelled beetles about $3/8$ inch long. Immature potato bugs are soft, reddish, humpbacked forms about $1/2$ inch long. Both adults and the young feed on tomato leaves.

Controls: Hand-picking is a good control, as is crushing any eggs found on leaves. Dusting with Rotenone also works. Plant tomatoes away from potatoes if possible.

Potato Psyllids

Shorter than $1/8$-inch-long jumping insects, these are tan to brown in color. Potato psyllids feed on foliage, causing the leaves to roll and become yellow or purple. They also stunt plants and deform fruit. They are general everywhere in the United States but most severely on the eastern slope of the Rocky Mountains.

Controls: Remove infested foliage by hand where possible, or use the spraying controls recommended for aphids. Again, don't plant tomatoes near potatoes.

Puffiness

Puffiness, or pockets, is a condition that results in hollow, soft, and lightweight fruit. When puffy fruits are cut, large air pockets are found in the cavities normally occupied by seed-bearing tissues. No decay or discoloration follows as a result of puffiness, but the fruits are a poor, unusable quality.

Controls: Plants may produce normal fruit later in the season. Avoid high nitrogen fertilizers and keep soil evenly moist.

Purple or Bluish Leaves

This symptom usually indicates a phosphorus deficiency, especially when coupled with spindly plants.

Controls: May correct itself as the soil warms. Top dress around plants with compost or a general-purpose fertilizer.

Rabbits

Rabbits have little interest in tomato fruits but may nibble on young plants.

Controls: Cover young plants with floating row covers or wire cages to protect them.

Raccoons

Raccoons are connoisseurs of ripe fruits, and technically tomatoes are fruits. They tend to harvest ripe fruits just the night before you planned to. They may sometimes dig up transplants because they smell like humans, and humans mean food.

Controls: If they are a real problem, you can try hanging a transistor radio in your garden—raccoons dislike loud noises, but so might your neighbors. Lights left on in the garden also scare them off. Raccoons are sometimes discouraged by garlic cloves left around plants and cayenne pepper sprayed on plants.

Septoria Leaf Spot

A fungal disease that attacks plant foliage, blemishing it with gray-centered, water-soaked spots and eventually causing almost all foliage to fall off, septoria leaf spot is most common during wet weather.

Controls: Remove and destroy infected leaves at once. Make sure to soak the soil and keep the leaves dry when watering. Keep the garden free of refuse and decayed plants; this can spread the disease.

Slugs

These slimy, soft-bodied, snail-like creatures are members of the mollusk family and voracious night feeders. Slugs feed on tomato foliage and even on fruit near the ground. They hide under rocks, boards, mulch, and other objects in the daytime and travel at night, leaving an oozy path.

Controls: Carefully inspect the garden, especially under rocks, mulch, and other objects, and destroy any slugs you find. You can also trap slugs by setting out dishes of stale beer, vinegar, or juice buried into the ground. A circle of dry sand, diatomaceous earth, ashes, sawdust, or hydrated lime around plants will help keep them away, since they dislike treading over these abrasive materials. Renew it after heavy rain. The best way to keep slugs at bay is to keep a clean garden bed and clean edge. Keeping plants staked also helps, as do coarse, scratchy mulches like hay. Groups of plants, raised beds, or container gardens may be protected by encircling the bed or container with a strip of copper pressed into the soil or tacked to the outside. Slugs won't cross copper—evidently it gives them a shock. Make sure nothing hangs over and touches the ground outside the copper barrier, or the slugs will use it as a bridge to dinner. Commercial slug bait poisons are also available. Use with extreme caution, as they may harm small children and pets.

Snails
Snails are slugs with shells.

Controls: *See Slugs.*

Spotted Wilt
This viral disease causes a bronzing of the leaves, made up of many tiny dead spots on the young top leaves. The tips of the stems show dark streaks and ripe fruits have numerous large, raised spots consisting of alternate concentric rings of yellow and red. The spotted wilt virus is transmitted by thrips from infected flowers, vegetable, and weeds.

Controls: Keep the garden weed-free; plant resistant varieties.

Squirrels
Squirrels sometimes bite into ripe tomatoes.

Controls: Try red pepper dust or commercial repellent.

Stalk Borers
These medium-size (up to 1 inch long), yellowish, spotted worms bore into tomato stalks just above the roots causing the stems to topple. They are especially injurious to tomatoes in the southern United States.

Controls: Spray stems with Bacillus thuringiensis or Sevin (chemical). Hand-picking eggs on undersides of tomato leaves is also worth a try.

Stink Bugs
From a large family of insects, these bugs are variously marked with green, orange, white, brown, or black, and have a shield shape and an unpleasant aroma. Stink bugs are juice suckers that attack many vegetables.

Controls: Hand-pick them from plants or spray plants with garlic. Keep the garden clean of weeds.

Streak
A disease caused by a combination of several mosaic viruses, this causes dead areas to form along the veins in the leaves of the plants, and brown streaks to appear on the leaf stems and main stems. Dry, shrunken areas form on the green fruits.

Controls: Pull up and destroy infected plants. Keep the garden weed-free; control insects.

Sunscald
This is fruit sunburn and is very common in the Southeast. Fruits are blemished with light-gray scalded spots that often rot.

Controls: Provide shade for developing fruit; don't prune off too much foliage. Try interplanting them with taller vegetables in very hot climates.

Tobacco or Tomato-Mosaic Virus

The most common viral disease of tomatoes, tobacco mosaic causes plant leaves to become mottled with yellow and green spots and rough in texture. The mottled areas often turn brown and die. Infected plants are usually stunted and bear few fruits. Tobacco-mosaic virus is carried by aphids and other sucking insects and over-winters in the roots of ground cherry, horse nettle, jimsonweed, nightshade, bittersweet, matrimony vine, plantain, catnip, Jerusalem cherry, and other related plants.

Controls: Pull and discard badly stunted plants. Spray plants with a mixture of half skim milk, half water. Clean hands and tools with the same solution before touching healthy plants. Control insects.

Tomato Fruitworms

Up to two-inches long, these are greasy, pale yellow to dark green or gray worms with darker stripes running lengthwise over their backs. Fruitworms eat into tomato fruits, moving from tomato to tomato. They are also called corn ear-worms or boll-worms and are particularly destructive in California and the South.

Controls: Hand-pick, spray with garlic or bacillus thuringiensis, or dust with Sevin (chemical).

Where fruitworms are a problem, don't plant tomatoes near corn.

Tomato Hornworm

The tomato hornworm is a giant, up to 4 inches long, green, white-barred worm with a harmless thornlike horn projecting from its rear. It's probably the biggest and ugliest bug in the tomato patch. Hornworm adults are large hawk moths. Tomato hornworms are ravenous eaters of tomato fruits and leaves, and their damage is easy to spot: Leaves are mere skeletons when they are through. Hornworms usually deposit their eggs on the undersides of leaves.

Controls: Hand-pick adults and squash the eggs. Don't hand-pick any hornworm with white eggs attached along its back; they will hatch and kill the hornworm, and live on to lay more eggs on another hapless hornworm. Dill makes a good trap plant because the creatures are easier to see in the lacy foliage. Basil or borage planted next to tomatoes will repel hornworms. Spray plants with bacillus thuringiensis or a chemical pesticide.

Verticillium Wilt

A common, soil-borne fungal disease, it attacks the leaves and vascular systems of the tomato plant, weakening it and reducing yield. The first symptom is yellowish splotches on the lower leaves in the center of the plant. Soon chocolate-brown spots develop in the middle of the yellow area and the plants drop some lower leaves.

Midday wilting and evening recovery is common. Careful inspection of a slit stem near the soil line will show tan streaks just under the skin. This dead tissue prevents proper transport of food and water to and from the root system.

Controls: Pull and destroy infected plants. Clean up all debris in the fall. Don't dig potatoes or tomatoes, or their foliage, into the garden, since they can harbor the disease. Plant resistant varieties.

Weed Killer Injury
Tiny amounts of common weed killers (herbicides) such as 2,4-D and 2,4-5-T can injure tomato plants, causing leaves to twist and fruit to become cracked, catfaced, or cone-shaped. Take great care when applying these weed killers near tomatoes. Stricken plants may outgrow the problem if the damage was light.

Controls: Avoid the problem in the first place: Don't use weed killers near tomatoes.

Whiteflies
Whiteflies are small, white, mothlike flies which flutter out in clouds when disturbed, and thus are popularly referred to as "flying dandruff."

They are most often a problem for greenhouse and indoor plants, but whiteflies feed on the leaves of tomato plants.

Controls: If they are a problem in the garden, try planting mint or tansy around tomato plants to repel them. Garlic sprays are also effective. In the greenhouse, the parasite Encarsia formosa is often introduced to feed on whiteflies and is very effective.

Woodchucks
Woodchucks are large, slow-moving vegetarians. They may occasionally develop a taste for young tomato plants.

Controls: Cover young plants with floating row covers or wire cages to protect them.

Y Virus
A serious virus disease, it results in the yellowing of younger leaves, drooping plants, and purplish streaks on stems. It is carried by aphids from infected potato plants to other plants in the garden.

Controls: Remove infected plants. Control aphids. Plant potatoes and tomatoes away from each other.

The ladies in Burpee's customer service department answering mail at the turn of the century.

Chapter 7

Gardeners' Most-Asked Questions

The first Burpee catalog was mailed in 1876, and the catalogs have been coming ever since, offering gardeners a wealth of seeds, plants, fruits, shrubs, and trees, as well as advice for better gardening. From the earliest years, Burpee has received letters from customers describing their gardens and asking questions. Today our "Gardening Hot Line" receives over 35,000 phone calls a year and here are some common questions about tomatoes.

Opposite: *The ladies in Burpee's customer service department answering mail at the turn of the century.*

GETTING STARTED

Q: *When should I plant my tomato plants out in my garden?*

A: Tomatoes are hot-weather plants, and they will sulk if you plant them out before the weather is settled. Wait until both air and soil temperatures average at least 60°F over twenty-four hours. If you want earlier harvests, you can set them out up to 4 weeks earlier if you protect the plants from the cold conditions. See page 62 for more information on growing early tomatoes.

Q: *I want to start my own tomato seedlings, but I'm never sure when to start them so they are ready to set out at the right time. When should I start them?*

A: Tomato seedlings should be about seven to eight weeks old when you plant them out in your garden. You can easily determine local planting times by calling your state agricultural extension service or by consulting experienced local gardeners. Count backward from that date to find out when to plant your tomato seeds.

Q: *When I buy a packet of seeds, there are always lots more seeds than I need. Will they be any good if I save them for next year, or do I need to buy fresh tomato seeds every year?*

A: Tomato seeds usually germinate pretty well one or even two years after the year for which they were packaged, if they are stored properly. Store your leftover seeds in a cool, dark place in a sealed glass jar with an inch of dry milk or silica gel in the bottom to absorb excess moisture. Many gardeners buy some new varieties of seed each year, and plant leftover seeds of other varieties. If you are counting on a specific variety, of course, it is always safest to buy fresh seed.

Q: *Help! The mail carrier left my seed order sitting on my porch, and it's below freezing. Will my seeds be okay?*

A: As long as the seeds were still dry and in their packets they should be just fine.

Q: *My tomato seedlings are growing tall and spindly, and the leaves are pale. What's wrong?*

A: Tomato seedlings need lots of strong, direct light. If you are growing your plants on a windowsill, place them as close to the glass as you can without touching it. Choose your sunniest window. Turn the seedlings daily so they don't bend way over toward the light. Brush gently across the tops of the seedlings with your hand once a day to encourage stocky growth. If none of your windows get full sun for most of the day, you will need to use lights to grow stocky seedlings. See page 57 for tips on selecting and using plant growth lights. Be sure to adjust the height of the light every few days to keep it about one inch above the topmost leaves, or place the plants on a pile of newspapers and remove the newspaper layers to keep the leaves at the proper distance from the lights.

GROWING

Q: *My tomato plants are growing enormous, and look remarkably healthy, but I don't see very many flowers and even fewer fruits. What should I do?*

A: Chances are your plants are suffering from excess nitrogen fertilizer in the soil, causing them to grow lots of stems and leaves, but very few flowers. Don't give them any more nitrogen-rich fertilizer, and they will probably start to bear fruit after they use up the excess. Pruning off some branches will speed up the process. You might even let some weeds grow up around the plants to soak up some of the extra nitrogen, and then pull them out.

Q: *I don't have much time to fuss with my tomatoes; what's the easiest way to grow a few plants?*

A: Most gardeners agree that black plastic mulch and sturdy wire tomato cages make growing tomatoes quite easy and carefree. Prepare your tomato patch (or even a large container) by loosening and enriching the soil, spread a layer of black plastic mulch over it, and plant seedlings through holes cut in the plastic. Press a sturdy wire cage over each seedling, making sure it is firmly anchored, and stand back. The tomatoes will grow up inside the cage with no tying or tucking, and the plastic will all but eliminate weeding chores. Just keep the soil moist at all times (a drip irrigation system installed under the plastic and a shut-off timer can make this a one-minute task every few days), and soon you'll be harvesting your own juicy, low-work tomatoes.

Q: *My tomatoes are really oddly shaped, and many have black patches on their bottom ends. Why?*

A: Early in the season, misshapen tomatoes may be caused by cold damage to the flowers. This should clear up as the season progresses. Some "heirloom" varieties are ribbed and contorted by nature, not baseball-shaped like more modern varieties. The black patches at the blossom end are probably due to "blossom end rot," a condition related to uneven soil moisture and low calcium levels in the plant. Keep the soil evenly moist to help prevent this problem.

Q: *Why do my tomato fruits crack?*

A: Tomato fruits crack when the roots soak up water faster than the fruit's skin can grow to accommodate it. This often happens after a heavy rain or a heavy watering if the soil was allowed to dry out beforehand. Keep soil evenly moist to help prevent this problem.

Q: *My plants are outgrowing their supports. What can I do?*

A: If the existing stakes or cages are standing firmly, just splice another section of stake or cage to the top of the existing support. Overlap it at least one foot, and secure it firmly with wire ties or strapping tape. If the plant is threatening to topple the existing support, pound a longer, stronger stake into the soil six to eight inches away from the stem, and tie the plant loosely to the new support—or get a larger, sturdier cage, and press it firmly into the soil around the existing caged plant.

Q: *How do I tell if my tomato plants need water?*

A: Your tomato plants always need water. Your job is to keep the soil evenly moist at all times (moist does not mean soggy; moist soil feels like a well-wrung out sponge). The best way to do this is by frequent (every day or every few days), light waterings. If by chance the soil does dry out, water it slowly until it is evenly moist from the surface to at least a foot below the surface. Keep it that way with frequent, light waterings. See the section on watering in Chapter 2 for more tips and techniques on watering your tomatoes.

HARVESTING

Q: *How can I tell when my tomatoes are at the peak of ripeness? And how should I keep them once I pick them?*

A: A ripe tomato is fully colored, glossy, and just slightly soft to your fingers. Check your plants every day or so and pick the ripe ones, clipping the stems, or gently twisting them off while holding the main stem with your free hand. Once harvested, do not put them in your refrigerator (unless they have cracks or other damage, and you can't use them right away)—refrigeration robs them of taste and changes their texture. Store them at room temperature, or freeze, can, or dry them for future use.

Q: *There's a chance of frost tonight, and my plants are covered with plump, green tomatoes. Can I save them?*

A: Yes! You can protect plants from light frosts by covering them with old sheets or quilts. Remove the covers once things warm up in the morning. Full-size, but still green, fruits will continue to ripen after they are picked, so it's worth picking them all before the first hard frost. See page 39 for directions for ripening tomatoes indoors. Immature green fruits can be used in a number of recipes.

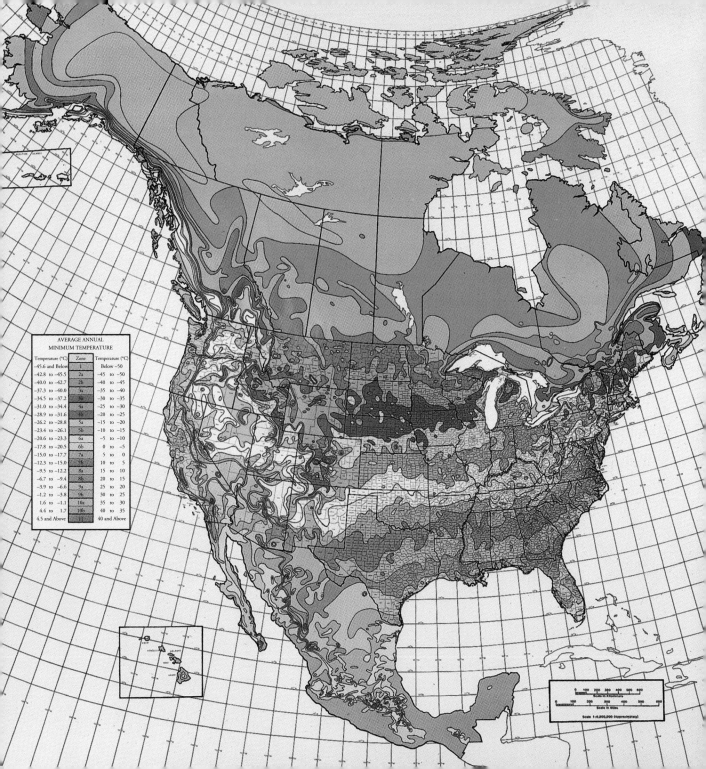

AVERAGE ANNUAL
MINIMUM TEMPERATURE

Temperature (°C)	Zone	Temperature (°C)
−45.6 and Below	1	Below −50
−42.8 to −45.5	2a	−45 to −50
−40.0 to −42.7	2b	−40 to −45
−37.3 to −40.0	3a	−35 to −40
−34.5 to −37.2	3b	−30 to −35
−31.0 to −34.4	4a	−25 to −30
−28.9 to −31.6	4b	−20 to −25
−26.2 to −28.8	5a	−15 to −20
−23.4 to −26.1	5b	−10 to −15
−20.6 to −23.3	6a	−5 to −10
−17.8 to −20.5	6b	0 to −5
−15.0 to −17.7	7a	5 to 0
−12.3 to −15.0	7b	10 to 5
−9.5 to −12.2	8a	15 to 10
−6.7 to −9.4	8b	20 to 15
−3.9 to −6.6	9a	25 to 20
−1.2 to −3.8	9b	30 to 25
1.6 to −1.1	10a	35 to 30
4.4 to 1.7	10b	40 to 35
4.5 and Above	11	40 and Above

Scale in Kilometers

Scale in Miles

Scale 1:6,350,000 (approximately)

Index